SWEET WINDS OF EGYPT

by Jeanette Pickering

Vabella Publishing

Vabella Publishing
P.O. Box 1052
Carrollton, Georgia 30112

Copyright © 2011 by Jeanette Pickering

All rights reserved. Except for brief quotes that may be used by a reviewer, no portion of any entry in this book may be duplicated or reproduced in any form, stored in any retrieval system or transmitted by any means in any format for any reason without written permission from this author.

13-digit ISBN 978-09834332-3-1

Library of Congress Cataloging-in-Publication Data

Pickering, Jeanette.
 Sweet winds of Egypt / by Jeanette Pickering.
    p. cm.
 ISBN 978-0-9834332-3-1 (pbk.)
 1. Egypt--Description and travel. I. Title.
 DT56.2.P53 2011
 916.2045--dc23
                                    2011038443

10 9 8 7 6 5 4 3 2 1

DEDICATION

I dedicate this book to my brother Larry Joe Sell, who all his life had wanted to go to Egypt. He was fascinated with its culture, its history, its antiquity. He was curious about its people and his dream was to meet them face to face, in their country.

My brother never got to live out his dream. He could have gone, he just never did. But he was happy that I got to go. Bro Joe died this year. Maybe in a way, I went for him.

TABLE OF CONTENTS

And So Begins the Ancient 1
Inside a Pyramid 4
Farming Egyptian Style 9
Pyramids, Tombs and Mastabas, Oh My! 14
Museums, Perfumeries and a Laser Show 18
A Ride Through the Nile Delta 22
Alexander the Great's Alexandria 26
A Swirling Egypt 30
Who's on for a Camel Ride? 34
Between the Sphinx's Paws 38
In the Chamber of a King 42
Meeting a Get-Down Pyramid Man 46
The Power of a Museum 50
Life on the East Bank and the West Bank 55
A Queen Who Would Be King 63
A Night Life with Bargains 67
An Unfulfilled Pilgramage 71
Boomerang 75
Balloon Ride on a Morning Wind 78
Unheard Words from Sekhmet 82
Holding My Hand 86
A Green Facial 90
The Graveyard of Kings 93
Temples, Tacking Sails and Tears 96
And the History Lessons Continue 100
The Woman in the Mirror 104
Lights and Sounds and Peeping Toms! 108
And So I Sing, Thank You 112
Homeward Bound 115

FOREWORD

Somehow I always knew my life would be blessed with unordinary adventures. Often I found myself choosing the less traveled path where the experiences led to exciting joys only I could feel.

Leaving college before graduating to be a teacher, I married a funeral director to join his calling and bear his four children. Forty seven years later he died. I decided to see the world.

My travels took me to New Zealand and Australia, Canada and Europe. Later I took a cruise through the Panama Canal and stopped in St. Thomas where I met a sailor. I married him two years later and at the age of seventy and he and I sailed the Caribbean Sea for eight years. While in Trinidad we lived on land for a year while we worked on the boat. We flew to Venezuela and traveled up into the Andes Mountains. Later we sailed the boat back to the Bahamas and ended up in Savannah, GA. The Captain sold the boat. We separated.

On my eightieth birthday I received a call from a sailing friend who had made plans to visit Egypt. She asked me to join her. Using another less traveled path, we made this unusual journey that I write about in this book. There are still less-traveled paths that await me. I know they are out there, and I'm ready whenever the call comes.

—Jeanette Pickering—

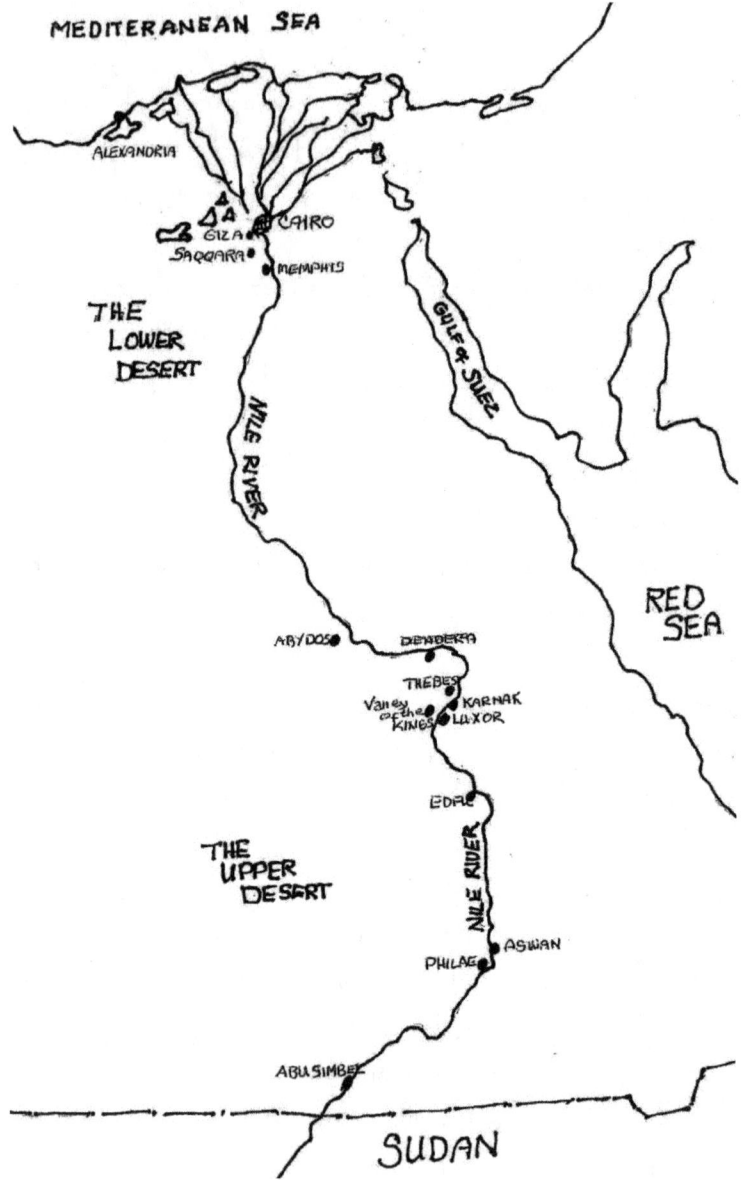

CHAPTER ONE

"AND SO BEGINS THE ANCIENT"

My sweet Buddy was totally unaware of how his life was going to be changed. He had excitedly hopped into the front floorboard of the passenger's side of my car and obediently laid down waiting for a ride. So it was with a twinge of shame that I left him with his new caretaker. Yet I was secure in the knowledge he would not be missing me at his new home for two weeks, for he would be joining the company of new canine friends.

My plane for Cairo would not be leaving until 10:00 tomorrow morning but I had chosen to drive to St. Louis today, spend the night in a hotel there and be refreshed for the twenty plus hours of flight time tomorrow.

I spent a restless night fighting the anxiousness of boarding the American Airlines Flight at an early 6:00 am. But all was well as I flew the first leg of the journey. At the transfer gate in New York Airport I joined my old friend Terry, whom I had met in Trinidad eight years ago. We had shared many boating experiences in the Caribbean and now it was meant to be that we share another adventure together. But this time it would be in the sands of the Egyptian desert as opposed to the clear seas of the Caribbean.

1

Sweet Winds of Egypt

The flight from New York was long and uncomfortable. And no matter how hard I tried, I could not sleep. The back side of the seat in front of me held a small screen and with the press of a button, a map would appear showing a line with the symbol of a plane in front of it which marked the route we were taking. We followed the flight over the Atlantic Ocean, watched the plane symbol as it crossed the country of France, down the Aegean Sea, and cross the toe of the boot of Italy. We crossed the southern tip of Greece and across Crete to Cairo on the Ancient Nile. Because it was nighttime we were unable to see from the windows any of the lands or waters we had crossed.

We were greeted at the Cairo Airport by a tour representative who drove us through the twelfth largest city in the world, a city of fifteen and a half million people. We had arrived at evening time so I was able to observe them going about their daily way of living. I quietly began to get a feel of these people; who they were, the way they lived. But it would not be until later that I would reach them on a more personable level. Those of us on the tour that had arrived at the airport at this same time were taken in a small bus to the very old Mena House Hotel. Upon entering a quiet, cool room in this place full of rich history, I promptly lay down to catch my breath and just rest a bit. The trip had been exhausting for me. Now that many of the rules of the airlines have been changed I had been stressed with the push of those changes.

Jeanette Pickering

Later Terry and I shared an evening meal with Lisa who had also been on the plane. We ate in the Hotel restaurant where we were first introduced to the strange, yet so delicious food of this area of the world. A small group of Egyptian businessmen were eating at a table near us. I was mesmerized by their soft spoken language.

An early bed time for me tonight was almost mandatory. Walking across the marble tiled floors, carpeted by old Egyptian rugs, I rode the elevator up to the eleventh floor taking the twists and turns to get to the long, high ceilinged hallway. Then walking on more elegantly carpeted floors I passed under heavy wooden archways placed at intervals along the corroder searching for room, # 1118. Entering a room that held a comfortable eighteenth century aura, I let my mind slip back in time. The bed was soft and inviting. And with a quick change into my night gown I settled down to get a good night's rest.

Cairo, Egypt

CHAPTER TWO

"INSIDE A PYRAMID"

Despite having four months in which to watch videos, read a number of books in an attempt to correlate all of it with the presentation brochure "Time and Space" which had been sent to me from Ruth, the owner of our ALL ONE WORLD Tour Company, I left the Mena House Hotel this morning as ignorant and awkward as a second grade student. What I soon found out was that to absorb over 5,000 years of history in the span of two weeks is ridiculously impossible! It took me a few days to even be able to recognize that.

I plunged in with an excitement of focused dedication to learn the secrets I felt Egypt had to tell me, using facts and hieroglyphics mixed with ancient fantasies. Eventually, just being here, moving among these pleasant Egyptians, there came a feeling of floating back into a time so ancient that sometimes it played tricks with my mind.

The second day began with an elegant breakfast buffet and a half-hour of introductions shared by the eighteen of us who would soon become bonded friends. On our way to the bus I chatted a bit with Tim who had told us he was from Denver. "I have a nephew who lives in Denver" I volunteered. "He has worked as a paramedic for many years, lately working from the Denver Airport facility.

He plans to retire soon. His family and I sailed through the British Virgin Islands ten years ago."

And then you could have bowled me over with a feather, for he replied "Cliff has already retired. He, his wife Chris, and a group of us are planning to go sailing there this spring." It seems that Tim had seen my name, Pickering, on the roster and wondered if I could possibly be a relative of his friend. But he had shrugged it off as being too far fetched. Amazing! Now what are the chances of this happening?

Using the Mena House in Giza, a suburb of Cairo, as our base for a few days, we traveled by bus southward towards the pyramids in Dashur. Even though we could see the complex of the Great Pyramids from our hotel rooms, we would not visit them until a few days later. The ones we would visit today are older, being built during the time of the Old Kingdom by King Sneferu during the 4th Dynasty of Pharaohs, approximately during the years of 2613 to 2589 B.C. My mind struggles with the concept of such a long passage of time for these man-constructed edifices to have survived in such good shape.

Our teacher and guide, Ruth, endeared herself to us with her humorous, intelligent and wise manner of explaining these antiquities as we examined them first hand. We let ourselves flow into the reality of the human beings who lived in those times, the way they constructed their thoughts, seeing that they behaved and approached life in much of the same way as we do today. The love and spirit of family was important to them also. They manifested a religion of Gods and Goddesses that lasted through centuries. They erected memorials that even today baffle the minds of engineers.

Yet as we moved from place to place, absorbing the past, the present was always with us. On our bus and always staying close by was an armed security guard. You knew he was there, dressed in his black business suit and tie. It was obvious that the protrusion under his jacket was a big gun carried in the holster around his waist.

Our Egyptologist guide, one of the handsomest silver haired Egyptians you would ever want to meet, led and taught, teased and totally endeared himself to all of us. With his accented English, interspersed with the clicks and chugs of his native Arabic tongue, he shared all we could absorb of his vast knowledge of his beloved land and its ancient inhabitants.

This day was so full, so overwhelming, that my mind found itself in overload even before the noon meal. Dashur is many miles south of the Giza Pyramids and far enough away from the in-and-out tourist destinations that we had the chance to begin our savoring the riches of Egypt without the crowds and the hordes of souvenir sellers we would later encounter on our trip.

The bus pulled up to an open desert area where three pyramids stood, having been built centuries apart. Stepping out into the dry desert air we got our first feel of the ancientness of this land. Ehab Mahmoud ushered us across a short space of sand and up the side, 140 steps, to the small entrance of the Red Pyramid. On the bus we had looked at a diagram of the innards of this monstrous sandstone block structure which showed a long ramp down and then a long distance across into the burial chamber of King Sneferu. Looking down from the small entrance into that dark shaft, lit only here and there along the narrow, low ceilinged tunnel, I gulped in wonderment. With a beating-heart fear caused by my semi-claustrophobia, I questioned if I would be able to make the journey required to enter that tomb that once held the mummy and possessions of an ancient ruler of Lower Egypt.

But there was no time for deliberation. Already living on 10 years of borrowed time, I quickly decided that if my life should come to an end here, this would be a fantastic place to close it out! So I ducked my head and followed these new, young whipper-snapper friends of mine down the ramp of 240 stepping boards into the hot and stuffy inner tomb, then up another 30 or so steps onto a platform that overlooks an unfinished chamber which would have been the burial chamber if it had been used. The burial chamber in the Bent Pyramid is finished off beautifully so it is assumed that the Pharaoh was probably buried there instead.

I was so overwhelmed by it all. Here I was, inside this small enclosure, surrounded by tons and tons of limestone blocks. Yet the excursion wasn't over yet. I still had to climb back down the 30 and back up the 240 steps.

Sweet Winds of Egypt

If you are wonder just how I know how many steps I took, I had to use counting them as a way to keep my heart from jumping out of my throat and my mind from popping out of my ears. I was never so glad in all my life as I was when I saw the blue sky again and was able to breathe the clean desert morning air. And to know I was still alive. Yet still there was so much more to come.

Giza, Egypt

CHAPTER THREE

"FARMING EGYPTIAN STYLE"

Our guide, Ruth, doesn't do things half-way. This woman goes all out! A trait that makes her Tours the best in all of Egypt. For following her firecracker introduction to the Pyramids, she invited us to actually tread the sands of her dry, open desert. With each of us going at our own pace, some stepping faster ahead of those walking in small groups at a normal speed, there were a few of us who poked along filling our pockets with the small, uniquely formed pebbles that were mingled in with the white grains of sand.

The desert, in Ruth's explanation of it, is rich with inspiration, and the vastness of it is exhilarating. We walked almost a mile south of the Red Pyramid to the Bent Pyramid, also built by King Snefru. We know all this because of an extraordinary discovery by a French engineer named Bouchard who in 1799 while repairing the outer wall of Fort Julian near the city of Rosetta, found a black granite stone that contained inscriptions written in Greek, Demotic and Hieroglyphs. It was a code to use in deciphering the ancient writings. Thus men are now able to interpret the hieroglyphs that were painted inside the pyramids.

Sweet Winds of Egypt

It was a long walk. I had neglected to bring my hat for protection from the sun's hot and quickly burning rays. Ruth loaned me the lavender scarf she was wearing around her neck, tucking it around my head and face in Bedouin fashion.

Through the years a number of the limestone blocks close to the bottom edge of this oddly bent pyramid had crumbled and fallen creating an overhang that gave us a shady spot to rest. In the snapshots we took as we cooled ourselves in the ever present moving breezes, I looked like one of the older wrinkled, dry skinned native women. And strangely enough, I felt quite comfortable here as if this could even be my home.

We were unable to enter this structure which because of its shape is called the Bent Pyramid. It was built during the time of the Old Kingdom but was the key center of worship during the Middle Kingdom. We were also able to view in the distance the Black Pyramid which was built in the years of the Middle Kingdom, fashioned from mud bricks. I was amazed to learn that over 110 pyramids have been discovered in these desert sands.

Back on the bus, still accompanied by Mr. Ramadan, our security guard who had dutifully accompanied us on our desert walk, we drove back north to the Saqqara area where some friends of Ruth have a farm in what is called the Black land (as opposed to the Red Lands of sand). They welcomed us for lunch in their guesthouse. We were served food that had been specially prepared for our weak American stomachs by washing and cooking everything in bottled water. The bacteria in these Egyptian waters are foreign to our bodies and must be avoided. We never drank tap water. We didn't even rinse our toothbrushes in it.

Our meal consisted of baked eggplant, cabbage rolls with rice, green peppers and rice, served along side of baked fish and tiny pigeons, potato and tomato casserole with pita bread and fresh dates. My, oh my! A pyramid crawl can make one quite ravenous!

We toured their farm which they had named Blue Lotus because of the lovely little pond filled with blossoming blue lotus plants in the tiny courtyard behind the house. The farm plots are divided by canals in which water from larger canals, pumped in from the Nile irrigate their crops. The workers live poverty filled lives yet seem to have a contented and happy nature. We shared gifts of clothing, ball caps and sweets we had brought with us from the States. They seemed so appreciative of our gifts. My roommate, Terry had brought long cotton socks for the women (it can get very cold here in the winter months) and they were delighted.

They farm the land with the use of donkeys, water buffalo and camels. Quoting one of the Egyptians, "If you want to learn about ancient Egypt, study the traditions of the local farmers." They may well be the closest link we have to the ways of the ancients.

Sweet Winds of Egypt

On leaving the farm we visited a local Carpet School where they create folkloric scenes on rough wool carpets, make Persian style carpets and also create intricate, tiny knotted silk rugs of beautiful designs and values. I purchased a small silk one, so beautiful it took my breath away.

Later in the afternoon as we continued north on our return back to the Cairo area, we visited a sight that is not open to the general public. Again we were able to avoid the crowds we would soon enough be introduced to. We were given a special permit to enter the site of the Niuserre Sun Temple in an area at Abu Gurab. At one time this site contained temple buildings and an obelisk, which were later destroyed. Remaining however is the central alabaster altar which represents the sun, surrounded by blessings in four directions. It was on this round altar where a few of us had climbed, or in my case had to be boosted up onto, that we sat with joined hands and meditated on the power that had once emanated from this worshipful area thousands of years ago. This would become the first of many meditation sites experienced by those of us who chose to do so.

Five of our group had made previous Egypt tours with Ruth. One of them, Rosanna, wanted to return to do a bit of extended research on these ancient structures. She was especially interested in the process the ancients used in the cutting of the enormous slabs and obelisks from the quarries and the tools that would have cut them. She had contacted and urged the original group to come back for another search. Those who did were dubbed "Boomerangs". It was at this site she did find some evidence of saw-blade cuts on the huge alabaster stones.

Our final excursion for the day (whew!) was a visit to a gold shop which sold not only basic Egyptian jewelry resembling the necklaces and bracelets of the Pharaoh Kings and their Queens, but both silver and gold cartouches that depicted your name written in hieroglyphics. What else could I do? I will probably never be in Egypt again so why not? I had a silver one made with my first name, Naida, formed in its oblong oval. I will wear it until my demise when it can then be passed along to my namesake granddaughter.

Needless to say it was sweet to drive up to the grand doorway of the 5-star Mena House and ride the elevator to the eleventh floor, there to shower and DROP into a sweet, soft bed, fading off into dreams of meeting old Pharaohs and young Queens on a wondrous journey back in time.

Giza, Egypt

CHAPTER FOUR

"PYRAMIDS, TOMBS AND MASTABAS, OH MY!"

And I thought yesterday was a busy day. I have only touched the hem of the Egyptian ancient garment, realizing I will be deciphering her secrets for days and weeks to come. Yet every moment of my adventure in the present was at one time, thousands of years ago, a similar adventure for some other human being.

As I now write of my experiences with hindsight, I pull it together by using the books I bought and the location maps of the pyramids. I revisit in my mind all the temples and tombs as I look through my pictures and the charts of Historical Dates. This second involvement in my spiritual walk back in time is nearly as exciting as the first.

Because of the physical logistics of reaching these historical locations, we are required to bounce back and forth as we visit places that were built during the time between 3000 BC and 600 AD. And that's more than a mere hop, skip and jump. But I must give credit to our Ruth who in 1996 knew she "needed to go to Egypt" and who absorbed herself into "feeling Egypt" in such a way that she could assimilate a pattern of touring that could let her guide others to as many historical sites as she could in a small allotted amount of time. I shall always be grateful to her for that.

On my third day in Egypt the first site chosen for our explorations was a compound called Saqqara which was fairly large and contained pyramids, tombs and mastabas. And then close by, we were able to check out the recently built Imhotep Museum which houses many of the statues and artifacts that have been moved from the complex for security reasons. This archeological site has structures built during all eras from the Third Dynasty onward. The compound is found in the desert just west of the old capital of Memphis. The famous Step Pyramid was built by King Zoser who ruled during the years 2649-2630 B C. This was a few years before the Dashur Red Pyramid was constructed, the one I crawled through yesterday. It was completed during 2575 -2465 B C. by King Snefru.

By keeping the places I visit in a chronological dating order it is easier for me to receive the total impact of its ancientness. This complex was created by people laboring at different jobs, then returning to their families at the end of the day to live lives quite similar in obligations to family and government as we do in the present. With all these thoughts in mind I find myself completely fascinated with all the things I see and am learning.

The tombs, temples and pyramids all fit into the funerary history of Egypt and concentrate mostly on their beliefs of death and afterlife. In this Saqqara complex one could easily spend a month and still not see it all. Its major attraction is the "Wedding Cake" pyramid historically named the Step Pyramid. It is the oldest structure in the world entirely built of stone. It was discovered in 1821 by a German archeologist. When the sand had been removed they found that this was not only a burial place of many Kings but contained the mastabas and tombs holding the mummies of the nobles and dignitaries who served them. There was a burial chamber for the High Priest Kagemni and one for the superintendent of the city, Mereruka. One tomb was known as "The Tomb of Doctors" where many of the engravings showed stories of their surgeries, one clearly outlining the ritual of circumcision. We even found one for Ptahhotep, a vizier and judge. As we viewed the impressively decorated paintings and relief engravings we could see how they described in minute detail the daily life in ancient Egypt.

    By the time we had wandered through the courtyards, hundreds of digital pictures had been snapped by the mere handful of us in our group as we fought our way through the courtyard clamor of a thousand other tourists. And my guess was that there were two vendors for every one tourist. A busy, busy place.

    Many times humor was the prevailing sanity-keeping factor. One of the vendors, wearing a long over-garment and head dress, removed his turban scarf to place it on Tim's head, asking for someone to take a picture of them. (Then they always ask to be rewarded with baksheesh, a tip). Another vendor got in the picture by putting his turban on Alex's head. A third one exchanged his head covering with Terry's. And thus the swapped cultural joviality had us all laughing at the fun.

The sun had begun to heat the sand to an unbearable temperature. As a last special treat we were allowed to enter the newly opened mastaba of Niankhkhnum and Khnumhotep, the twin brothers who were both priests of RA in the Temple of Niuserre that we visited yesterday. These men had been responsible for the "care of the hands of the Pharaoh". People who were the hairdressers and the manicurists, even the fan bearers and trusted servants, or anyone who was allowed to be in the King's presence and to "hear everything he had to say" were classified as privileged and rewarded with tombs and mastabas to honor them.

It was nearly noon, time indeed for a rest-room break and a bottle of cool water to wash down the sand grit from between our teeth.

Saqqura, Egypt

CHAPTER FIVE

"MUSEUMS, PERFUMERIES AND A LASER SHOW"

Many of the recent archeological excavations of the desert sands of Egypt were done in the 18th and 19th centuries by Europeans who were fascinated and fixated on culling out the secrets of the ancients, buried for thousands of years. Yet when they discovered them they also found that long before they had come, local robbers and thieves had stolen the mummies and the treasurers that were contained in these enclosures. What few unopened ones remained were then claimed by the European discoverers and carried off to the museums in their countries. Today there is an on-going request by the Egyptian government to have those antiquities returned.

So many were taken from the Saqqara complex. A limestone statue of a large sacred Apis bull once rested in an underground gallery called the Serapeum, but it can now only be viewed at the Louvre in Paris. The Rosetta stone, once held by the French and later taken by the British is now in a museum in England. Even the bronze ex-voto of Imhotep that was made during the Ptolemaic Period is in the Louvre in France and not in the small, new Imhotep Museum near the Valley Temple that bears his name.

Jeanette Pickering

Imhotep was a man that was classified by his people as one of the greatest geniuses in the history of mankind. He was an architect, a magician, and a philosopher. He became such a great Doctor that Greek history has identified him with Asclepius, their God of medicine. He is attributed to discovering how to cut stone for the buildings of their monuments. His name means "he comes in peace" and so it was in peace that we entered the lovely, cool, new building that now contains what few amazing artifacts have been salvaged from the adjacent Saqqara complex. It has been hinted that in a few days we might have the opportunity to hear from the present overseer of the excavations concerning some recent discoveries that have been made by the use of new laser equipment and maybe even sharing with us a real secret. With this teaser in mind we explored this well maintained building.

Our last stop for the day was at the Egyptian Perfume Palace where we were seated on low, comfortably backed benches and served our choice of tea, Turkish coffee or cola drinks. Now, relaxed and rested, we were treated to the aromatic delights of essences and oils being presented by a talented salesman and his lovely head-covered assistant who followed the Egyptian dress code only on her head covering. Her cosmetics and tight jeans were strictly western.

Perfume odors were shared with us by a touch on the wrist or back of the hand from a bottle stopper. We were given a listing of 24 aromatherapy oils and 52

Sweet Winds of Egypt

different essences from which to make a selection if we wished. Many of those in our group did choose to buy a fragrance or two. Because my friend Terry uses a lot of rose oil in her healing work, she purchased four large bottles which were packed in a beautiful blue velvet box. Little did she know that the new air flight regulations and requirements that the Egyptian government securities now make on checked liquids would cause a stressful delay in our admittance onto the plane for our return flight home.

I chose not to buy perfume but I did take a liking to the tiny, exquisitely designed cup and saucer that the coffee was served in. I asked if I could purchase a set of them. The salesman, ever ready to please, had one packed in bubble wrap and placed in a lovely little box. They were given to me at no charge. I was delighted.

I sat quietly off to the side waiting for a sweet young girl, who was not wearing makeup or Western clothing, go wash my cup and saucer and wrap it for me. When she returned, Ehab did not see me watching him as he slipped a small Egyptian bill into her hand as he took the box from her. Later I mentioned seeing him do it. "I only wanted to help her...she never gets tips for all her work behind what the customer sees. She has a family...."

This evening we were given an optional chance of traipsing around Cairo on our own or attending the Sound and Light Show at the amphitheatre near the Giza Pyramids. Terry and I and a few others chose the laser light show. So in a smaller bus with our trusted friend

Ehab and the usual armed guard, we joined tourists from all over the world. And how do I know they were from everywhere? Because the earphones that we used for the presentation had choices of over a dozen different languages. We listened in English and watched the colored laser lights hop from one pyramid to another, then to the sphinx, and then back to another pyramid.

It had been a long day. The evening air was warm and lulling. I had to fight dozing off to sleep. One of our group, Sweet John, a Kentucky boy who when he finally became a California man, caught himself a classy lady in Ms. Pat, thinks a bit like I do. I too came from a small town and these theatrics were just a little bit too much. As the English speaking commentator droned on monotonously, he wondered if listening to the presentation in Russian might have been a better choice. John's comment gave us a final bit of humor with which to end another lovely day.

Giza Egypt

CHAPTER SIX

A RIDE THROUGH THE NILE DELTA

The Tour brochure had listed this as a FREE DAY with four options; meaning free to choose between three different places to visit or just flop by the pool and rest. I wanted to choose all four.

Terry and I had agreed to stay together and she really wanted to see the city of Alexandria. So the tour of "Old Cairo" with its Churches, Citadel, Mosques and the Coptic Museum were out. And we would miss shopping with Ruth in the Avenue of the Tent-makers, the non-touristy area in Kerdesa. But our trip to Alexandria with three others of our group and our one-of-a-kind guide, Ehab, was in the end, the perfect choice.

The Cairo/Alexandria road was 220 kilometers long. They measure distance here in meters, not miles and I am so slow at figuring that I can't tell you how many miles that is. We were up at 5:30 and on the road by 7:00 to be able to see as much of the city as we could in the time we had. It was an eight lane highway, packed with traffic. We drove north-west, passing all manner of sights. On the south side, just outside Cairo, were the conclaves of fancy homes, dubbed "Beverly Hills". On the north side were miles and miles of building complexes of every major electronic business you could think of. It was dubbed the "Silicone Valley" of Egypt.

All the way across was delta farmland, much sandier than the land along the wide Nile River. Here they raised all kinds of crops, rotating them three times a year (they have four seasons just like we do, yet in ancient times they were divided into three because of the annual Nile flooding.) Besides cotton and rice, we saw hundreds of Nurseries growing date palms, trees of orange, olive, guava and mango fruit, ficus and other various shade trees, and grape vines, all of them watered from underground wells. Closer to Alexandria we saw salt flats, oil refineries and Gas companies plus a large prison compound. We also saw a few cattle and herds of goats.

One special curiosity kept showing up here and there beside the farm buildings. It looked like a huge beehive, covered with thousands of holes. I learned it was a huge bird house for pigeons, which are served as a delicacy here in Egypt.

We took a break-stop at an area similar to our highway rest-stops. In a coffee shop they were playing some neat music, definitely for the modern Egyptian teenager. I asked our bus driver if he could bargain for me in their language for that particular CD that was being played. He could, and did. Now I own a copy of Wayah's sultry songs with a picture of his "hunky" physique on the cover. Oh my...even with my eighty year old eyes he looks delicious!

Sweet Winds of Egypt

We had some wonderful adventures and discoveries while in Alexandria which I will describe in the next chapter but on our way back home one of those funny, humorous experiences of a language mix-up happened at another rest stop. It had been a warm day and we needed a cool-drink break. We chose to sit outside in the lovely patio. I was drowsy and decided to get a cup of coffee. I didn't want to go to sleep on the way home and miss something. The rest of the group got their colas and went outside. Toni and I tried to order coffee. It seems you are supposed to go up to the cashier and pay, and then you can give them your order. Only I didn't understand that. A nice young man finally figured out what I wanted, brought me my coffee and I paid him. He brought me back my change. It was a neat little coin with a hole in the center. Since I always try to bring home coins from the countries I visit, to share with my grandchildren, I tried to buy some more of the coins.

Oh, Lordy, what a mess. The young man thought I was saying he didn't give me enough change back, the manager got upset with the waiter and shoved him for not treating me nice....so before a fist-fight got started, I grabbed my coffee and got out of there. Toni had already gone outside and told the others I had started a fight and the only thing she could figure out was that they were fighting over her. We laughed all the way home. The next time I go to Egypt I am going to learn to speak their language first!

Jeanette Pickering

During the next few hours the six of us shared with each other, stories of our separate lives. We filled our cups to the brim with loving joy. On this day we became a family, and even though one might find it strange to understand, we meshed our lives and tied our knots into a beautiful Egyptian tapestry.

Alexandria, Egypt

CHAPTER SEVEN

ALEXANDER THE GREAT'S GREAT ALEXANDRIA

The city of Alexandria, even though it is an old city of nearly twenty three hundred plus years old, is still a spring chicken in the ancient lands of Egypt. Alexander the Great had come to Egypt in the year 332 B C and felt its geographical and historical great importance. As he passed through the area around a village named Rakoda, he decided to build a city on the island on the opposite side of it. This city would bear his name.

When he died at an early age his empire was divided among his commanders. Ptolemy's share was Egypt and until the year of 30 BC, his family ruled. Egypt was obligated to the Roman Empire and even became a Roman Province until the 7th century AD when the Arabs defeated them and the Islamic Era began.

The places we visited today were built, or as in the case of the Catacombs, were dug during the Roman Period. During this time the two empires were melded together. We saw this first hand on our first tour of the day.

We entered the Kom El-Shugafa Catacombs through a gateway of hired guards who searched our packs and bags for cameras. (Ehab had suggested that we leave them on the bus where the driver could watch them for they were not allowed inside the enclosure.) The underground tombs had been discovered in 1900 when a donkey accidently fell through the street, opening up a secret burial place hidden thousands of years ago.

These chambers were hewn out of solid rock on three superimposed levels and the dead were lowered down the central well of a spiral staircase (which we used to enter the tomb). The bottom opened up into an intricately adorned rotunda supported by eight carved pillars. The burial niches led off in spoke-like avenues. However, all the dead had for some reason been mysteriously removed years before the discovery.

It was a stuffy, creepy place that often had water seeping in under the plank boards that had been built for us to walk on. The planks were narrow and with all the tourist traffic that was coming and going, I was forced to again fight that claustrophobic feeling that comes over me.

Outside in the fresh air we sat drinking our bottled water as we talked about what we had just seen. Scattered around the seating area were some of the granite sarcophagus that had been used as bath tubs before they became burial caskets. This was a way weird thing yet quite a unique, economical recycling method of their time.

Our next jaunt was to the complex that contained a huge pillar that possibly was the burial place of Pompey as it carried his name. Its height is so tall it can be seen from the not too distant Mediterranean Sea. The base of the

Pillar was hewn from a huge pink granite rock, the same color as the plinth stone on which my already inscribed grave marker is set. However his marker is a bit classier than mine.

A couple of sphinx statues rest nearby a few subterranean galleries that once held the mummies of the sacred Apis bulls. There was also a room that some believe the unburned books from the ancient Alexandria library fire were once kept.

Our third stop was at the horseshoe shaped Roman amphitheatre complex, designated for listening to music. It was not a semicircle design that would be used for theatre. Most of us scattered to check out our own interests. Toni and I wandered down to the stage part of the 13 rows of white marble seats. There was another small group of tourists with their guide setting on the bottom row with one of the group standing in front of them on a small flat round circled stone embedded in the sandy stage area not six feet away from the audience. The guide was telling her to sing something and when she did she shrieked in amazement. No one else could figure out what had startled her. Then one by one the others tried it with the same results. After they left, Toni and I went over to see what it was all about. When I stood on the stone and sang or spoke, the echo penetrated into my head. It was the weirdest experience. And the second I stepped off the stone, still speaking, the vibrations stopped. Of course we had to share this with everybody that came by. Later the guide that we had stolen this experience from, saw me, chided and teased me saying "you owe me and my group a baksheesh!"

Putting our lunch on hold we chose to visit the world famous Alexandria Library. It was all and more than I expected. Three of our group were able to go into the sealed off area where the rare books were stored. Toni and I got lost and just wandered; enjoying the paintings and textile displays until our time ran out and we had to join the others to drive to the Qaitbey Fort by the sea. (Oh how I miss the sea!)

We then went to the "Fish House" where we shared a huge family style meal of elaborately prepared seafood and vegetables. What a delight, eating with forks and fingers, gathering up the left-over's in cartons for Ehab to share with a family who would appreciate them. Every day Ehab becomes a dearer friend.

As we left the city, Ehab had the driver make one more stop. A local pastry and sweets shop where he bought cookies and cakes and jelly candies for all of us to eat on our long bus ride home. What a way to end a day of sheer delight in this sweet new world of the Ancients.

Alexandria Egypt

CHAPTER EIGHT

A SWIRLING EGYPT

    Because of all the unrest in Egypt right now, I want to share with you a very personal incident of adventure that happened to me with these people who for a long time have been struggling for a better life. It happened on the evening of October 28th in the city of Cairo.

    This story was almost left out of the daily accounting of my adventures as it all had been an impromptu happening, one not included or planned in our normal itinerary. Someone had mentioned reading about the "Whirling Dervish" performers in Egypt. We wondered if they might be performing somewhere in Cairo. And mind you, Cairo is a mighty big city that has lots of entertainment opportunities for these people to enjoy. Their economy may be bad but they still need their entertainment.

    Ehab was our connection man. He knew of one particularly special group of young men who have performed their whirling act all over the world. They have been featured in film documentaries and they are good. They were to be dancing that evening at a small restaurant somewhere in an area where the ordinary middle class people come out, and I mean outside, to shop and eat and interact. I would like to call it a mall of shops without a roof, with people living in family apartments above the shops. It's hard to describe but it was like being at a big family get-together. Whole families came outside to socialize.

Six of us from our group chose to go. We were taken to this unfamiliar, yet friendly open place by our small bus. I can't recall if we had an armed guard this night for the guards had begun to blend in with our group just like they were a part of us. We had to walk a few blocks from where the bus dropped us off. It was simply delightful to walk among these people, being greeted by them, and then being promptly ignored as a third cousin coming to a pot-luck supper. "Hello. It's nice to see you." Kiss one cheek, then the other. "Now move on."

The restaurant was up on a third floor and the wooden staircase was like one inside of an old home with the rooms leading off into private shops where people lived behind their shops. It was so interesting. And there was a unique, truly modern Egyptian feeling about it all. Pharaohs and Tombs and Pyramids weren't a part of this, unless the shop might sell a trinket or two depicting them. This wasn't a tourist trap. This was where the Egyptians hung out.

We let Ehab guide us through the meal selection as he sat with us at our round table at the side of a long hall. Alcoves on both sides held tables and chairs where the locals had come to eat. I can't remember what we ate but it was delicious, being served by an older man with a young freshman waiter assisting him. The food was carried in from a door behind us and soon after we arrived the place began to fill up. It was quite noisy; a happy, sober noise. Alcohol is not openly sold or drunk in Muslim Egypt (except of course by the way of our Baptist-on-the-sly manner here in the U.S.). Toward the end of our meal, a group of about seven men entered from the serving area with a flute, a hand drum and a tambourine to play some strange (but only to us) music that seemed to pep up the spirits of the crowd. Later one older gentleman became the singer of the story that was told to us in their language. I wondered if these were the "Dervish" that would be dancing for us. They were dressed with their turbans and long white galabeyas. The one with the tambourine did a little twirl or two…but that was it.

    My cheap Timex watch had played out on me from the heat and desert dust. With no watch to mark the time, I found myself steeped as it were, in a teapot of the present moment. Any baggage of unsettledness that I may have brought with me from my world in Missouri dissipated as smoothly as a morning mist in the sun. Without fanfare four young men were suddenly there in this long room, wearing the colorful clothes of their whirling trade. And they immediately began their dizzy spinning that lasted what someone had determined to be fifty-two minutes, without stopping.

    It wasn't until they were half way through that I began to see this was not just a dance performance for them. They were in a hypnotic, religious ritual. Performing for us, yes, yet with their eyes lifted upward and hands reaching up and out to 'something other' than us.

I watched their colorful skirts. Sometimes one was being lifted over their head while a second layer blinked with battery operated colored lights. I watched their eyes, closing and opening, sensing the crowd, then oblivious to them. I watched their feet and realized it was the placement of them as they whirled that gave them the stability and equilibrium to keep them from becoming dizzy or falling.

The whole evening was one of an ether-world experience. It was an in-the-now experience for me at the time but as I look back on it, it is a blur. In fact, I ask myself, were there four young men or were there only three? They had seemed to meld into one unit that night.

It was here that I met the real Egypt. The people that most of us never get to see. Is it possible that some of those who were in that room that night were part of the crowd of people on the Cairo Square shown on our TV news networks only a month or so later?

Cairo, Egypt

CHAPTER NINE

WHO'S ON FOR A CAMEL RIDE?

The room I shared with Terry at the historic Mena Hotel on the outskirts of Cairo resonated an elegance befitting the long dresses and big hats worn by the European women of the 1800's who came with their 'suit and tie' gentlemen to climb into the Pyramids and Tombs long before floor planking and electric lights were installed. After they had made excursions like we took today, they must have truly enjoyed returning to the white marble floors and blue tiled bathroom walls to bathe and soak off the pyramid dust and desert sand.

The long corridor outside our room was comfortably wide with a tall ceiling, stretching nearly half the length of a football field. At intervals of about 100 feet, there were large wooden arches. Between the arches and flanking the walls were antique cabinets, tables and chests holding vases of fresh bird-of-paradise flowers. The only word to describe our accommodations would have to be "opulent".

Those of our group who were roomed on the opposite side of the hallway were able to view the three Giza Pyramids and the Sphinx. From our side the city sprawled out below us from our 11th floor view.

Jeanette Pickering

Our bus trip to the Giza plateau where we would spend most of the day was a quick one. We were not too far from the pyramid compound. Our first stop was at the Second Pyramid. Usually Ruth or Ehab would brief us on the history surrounding what we would be seeing each day. Because of the shortness of time our lesson was a quick one. I had to scribble my notes and then try to decipher them later. If I were to be tested on what I was taught today I'm sure I would have flunked. But by using the cheat notes given to us when we first came, I do know the approximate dates these pyramids were built. History books and the internet can present them in greater detail but I was satisfied in the brief details.

These pyramids were built by King Khufu (Cheops), King Khafre (Chephren) and King Menkaure (Mycerinus) between 2551 and 2472 BC. It's very hard to actually realize that they have survived that long, when you are standing there right beside them. It's when you creep inside them that your imagination becomes overwhelmed in trying to comprehend the enormous amount of labor that it took to create these huge burial places so many years ago.

Because we had come early we were able to avoid the crowds that would come later. We passed many waiting in line to purchase a ticket, who would be disappointed, for only a certain number of tickets to enter the pyramids could be sold. And Ruth had already purchased ours. We climbed up the outside stone steps to enter the second pyramid which still has its finished stone casing on the top which distinguishes it from the Great Pyramid build by King Cheops. Inside we walked down the wooden ramps with their cross boards to keep us from sliding. Down 65 steps, across a level space of about 40 yards and then up 91 steps. The farther we went in the hotter and stuffier it became. In the main chamber rested the King's sarcophagus. His mummy was no longer there.

Some of us took turns climbing in the granite container and laying down. Of course I had to give it a shot. I thought it might feel creepy but nothing tingled or transported me. I suppose if I had been there alone it might have. But there were too many people around for me to call up a Spirit.

The third Pyramid was closed so we were taken to the upper hillside overlooking the three pyramids where a professional photographer took a picture of our group charging $5. for an 8x10 photo. The price was right for it took a bit of skill for him to manipulate us into an empty spot in the horde of people who had by now gathered here to ride the camels.

With Ruth in charge and Ehab standing back with a smirk on his face, letting her deal with the camel men in charge of this full blown circus, she had things all worked out in a jiffy. It was a sight, seeing us climb on the camels backs to be bounced back and forth as they raised their long legs. Tied four in a row, we plodded down the hill, across a spot of desert and then back. Emmy, who raises horses in Vermont, wanted the reins to drive her own camel and was allowed to do so. She whapped him a little and got him to trot a bit. I was content to plod along in line and hang on to keep from falling off. The saddles on those camels were 'perty' high off the ground.

I had ridden a camel before when I was in Australia but that was twelve years ago. I am much smarter now about such things. I let the camel men lead my pseudo-steed. No fast ride for me. I chose not to break my neck today and spoil the rest of the trip. I've still got places to go and things to see before I call it quits.

Giza Plateau, Egypt

CHAPTER TEN

BETWEEN THE SPHINX'S PAWS

The first half of our fifth day in Egypt went quite well in the category of excitement. Crawling in a pyramid! Riding a camel! What next?

We were still on the Giza Plateau, some 50 meters above the Nile River. And it was getting noonish. (Interpret that as mighty hot!) A swim in the Nile would have been welcome. Instead we entered an air-conditioned Museum area at the base of the Great Pyramid to see a boat that may have sailed on the Nile at one time but was actually built around 2500 BC to carry King Cheops through his journey after death. This Solar Boat wasn't discovered until 1954. When it was uncovered from its stone chamber pit covered by sand, it was in remarkably good condition.

It had been dismantled before it was buried and was in 1224 pieces when found. Eighteen-ton slabs of stone had covered the long line pit. The boat when put together measured 143 feet long and was made of Lebanon cedar wood. This is probably why it had not rotted. Today in Missouri we use our cedar wood for our outside furniture as it also weathers well.

The boat was to be manipulated by huge leaf-end oars, quite large and long. I'm guessing 35 feet. The leaflike ends themselves were 7 feet long. It would have taken some very strong men to pull that boat into the afterlife.

    Seven boat pits have been found around the pyramids, some of them empty and one that has not yet been opened. Five were found near the Great Pyramid and two near the Queen's Pyramids. Inside the museum walkways had been built around the base where the boat was resting and also one on an upper level from where we could look down on the boat with its strangely shaped prow and stern. At the front of the boat there was a boxed place where one of the servants would stand with flags to direct the boat left or right. The stern was shaped like the hieroglyph for Ma'at. In the middle, behind the oars, was the 'cabin' where the king would have been. The craftsmanship was astounding.

    Leaving the Solar boat Museum we re-gathered at the outdoor café near the large amphitheatre from where we had viewed the Sound and Light Show. Eating the snacks we had either brought with us or something we purchased there, we sat in the shade from the hot desert sun and quietly absorbed the power of these ancient manmade creations in front of us.

    We walked across the compound to where the great Sphinx lay. The commotion from the hordes of tourists assaulted us until we reached the enclosure of the privacy fence around the carved stone man/cat. Our extraordinary Ruth had obtained, at no little expense, special passes that gave us two private hours in this enclosure, allowing us to descend into a space and time that reached all the way back into history. I chose to wander around alone, leaving my camera in its case and tying my mind to nothing except the ancientness of it all. I touched the stone of its large paws. I felt the swing of its large tail now wrapped up along its right side. I peeked into an inset on its left hind quarters. From the things I had learned, I knew that in the days that this huge edifice had been created, women would have been conspicuously absent from this area. Yet here I was. A woman, a privileged woman, seeking a small supply of its strength to aid me in the problems I would soon return to back home.

A few of our group met inside the funerary temple enclosure near the sphinx, making a circle of joined hands and letting whoever wished to place themselves in the center to ask for strength and uplifting from the others. I stepped into the center, covered my head and face with my white scarf and expelled in muffled sobs the pressure-filled tension I had carried to Egypt with me. I released it. I purged out the harbored disfavor and hurt of the past. Now empty I was ready to be slowly filled with something of a different kind. Something new. Something this ancientness could teach me.

Ruth then gathered us all together in the secluded space between the Sphinx's huge paws. As we sat on the sand or whatever ledge was available, she handed each of us a small pad and pen. With her soft spoken, meditative words she suggested we privately write down our thoughts of whatever commitments of purpose we were led to make to ourselves. They were not for sharing unless we wanted to. We all wrote but none of us was moved to share.

My written words, those that came from the enlightened heart that I had been given that afternoon, have been read numerous times since my return home. They seem to reassure me that my path is protected by the One Great God that King Akhenaten remained true to; nameless to him but whom I call "My Father".

Giza Plateau, Egypt

CHAPTER ELEVEN

IN THE CHAMBER OF A KING

Entering the Great Pyramid of Egypt is an extraordinary privilege. One of the Seven Wonders of the Ancient World, it is steeped with magical mysteries. Why would a mere man, great though he was in his time as the leader of the country of Egypt, feel the need to build such a labor intense, giant edifice just to have his mummified body rest in it for a desired eternity? What kind of an ego would command such an undertaking? This man, who had announced to his people that he had become a god, was known by the name of Cheops or Khufu. He never questioned his right or power to state his desire and command it to be done, nor did his people. He simply would say "Do it!" and it WAS done.

Long before our arrival at the entrance into this magnificent fete of workmanship, Ruth had applied for and received permission for our group of sixteen to enter after the 4:00 p.m. closing to the public. Special fees, possibly bordering on the rim of a requested baksheesh, passed through a few hands and when the last tourist straggled out into the late afternoon sunlight, we individually climbed the random step rocks up to the small entrance to a downward passage. As always, there was a dark skinned, older turbaned man, who would be wearing the common long skirted garment that was a dirty mayflower-blue color, waiting to tear off the stub-end of our tickets. Once inside we would do our hunch-walk, using the banisters that were fastened to the sides of the passageway.

We came to an intersection where one could choose to continue going farther on down five times as far as we had already come, into the subterranean chamber and a dead end passage. I wasn't even faintly tempted to try that experience. No way. Those young and dumb enough to try it, later rejoined our plod-along group with dust covered clothes and dripping with perspiration from crawling through pit passages that were unbearably stuffy and hot. So they said.

After climbing up a set of newly built steps, we made a sharp 90 degree right hand turn and then into a straight shaft that would lead us to the small room called the Queen's Chamber. It was in this cool room that we prepared ourselves for the drama to come. Many in our group were accomplished singers. Sensing the sounds we were making in this echo-conductive enclosure it seemed natural that we should sing. It started with spontaneous harmonic notes, hummed without rhythm. In a way it imitated some jazz sessions I've heard. Then with Ruth as a conductor without a wand, we were guided in sustaining a harmony hum that raised and lowered in volume. With a slight hand signal from her our voices became silent. Yet the vibrating echo spun through the chamber for a

Sweet Winds of Egypt

surprising amount of time before fading away. It was way too cool.

We had agreed that we would not speak aloud while we were in the King's chamber so as we walked back through the shaft taking us to the ramp that led us through the high vaulted Grand Gallery to reach the King's Chamber, we prepared for the silence that would follow. It had also been arranged that at 5:30 p.m. all the lights, dim though they already were, would be turned off for fifteen minutes.

We walked up the ramp in the Grand Gallery. With its pinnacled ceiling it held a magical majesty. The claustrophobic feeling that I had experienced before was not there. The Gallery served as a preview to the much larger and taller granite lined quarters for King Cheops's resting place. The chamber however, was empty save for a solid trough-like piece of mahogany colored granite. This was the King's outer sarcophagus. A large chip had been broken off at one end. The chip and its lid were gone as well as the King's mummified body.

Quietly, those who wished were helped up into the cold granite container where we each lay for a few minutes. Jim, who would be celebrating his birthday tomorrow, seemed to need and receive a special awakening of spirit and purpose as he took his turn to lie on his back as he reached up to hold his wife, Karen's outstretched hand. Earlier on I had taken my turn to lay in much the same position as the Pharaoh had lain. I was unable to sense any epiphany. There was no revelation, not even a moment of spirit. I guess King Cheops had nothing to say to me.

Just before the magical moment of 5:30, when the electricity was turned off, Pat, our theatrical critic, was taking her turn resting inside this rather spacious, lidless vault. Contrary to what one might think, never for a moment was any feeling of spookiness or fear felt by any of us, though some did experience what they described as power. We stood leaning or sitting against the wall, or as many did, laying flat on the cool floor with outstretched arms. Each of us crawled inside of ourselves and brought whatever god or spirit we wanted to inside with us.

As the light flickered back on, we maintained that rhythm of silence as we ascended back down the Grand Gallery to carefully step down the tight steps of stone and then back to the entrance doorway. The sun had set while we were inside and the evening air was fast cooling down. A simple spirit of peace had descended upon me, and in the light that was focused on the path by the waiting bus, Lisa took my arm and helped guide me to our transportation. I keenly felt her gesture of kindness.

The events of the day had sapped and drained away my energy. Too tired to even eat a bit of nourishment I quickly faded into sleep once I reached my lovely bed.

The Great Pyramid, Egypt

CHAPTER TWELVE

MEETING A GET-DOWN PYRAMID MAN

Back on our third day in Egypt, Ruth had hinted that we might be able to meet the honored overseer of the excavations at the large Saqqara complex we visited that day. And today it happened. Immediately after our breakfast we gathered in a secluded side room in the hotel where we were introduced to Ashraf Mohie el Din.

To me this Egyptian man epitomized the spirit of the old rulers of these ancient kingdoms. He was so sure of himself, almost to the point of arrogance. Yet according to Ruth, he has in his heart a hidden softness. Unmarried, he financially cares for his mother and extended family. Ashraf and his boss, who we often see on the Discovery and History Channels, are enough alike to be two peas in a pod.

It seems that many of the new inventions of man during our past decade have opened up opportunities for the examination of the hidden past, without destroying the physical treasures that are being uncovered. We are told that 70 % of the workmanship of thousands of years ago is still intact, still buried under the sands of this ancient country. The use of X-ray has helped decipher the name ownership of the hundreds of mummies stored in the famous Egyptian Museum here in Cairo. And a tiny camera-carrying robot has been used to peep into a hidden chamber located in the Great Pyramid. Only yesterday I had my picture taken standing by the side of the small wall shaft where the robot had entered, where it traveled back to a small 6" X 6" door. Then it threaded a camera through a pin hole it had drilled in the door, showing another hidden room. Amazing!

Still more discoveries are made. Now the use of Laser-light images has been used to aid archeologists in their new discoveries of more man-made formations under the tons of sand that has covered them for thousands of years.

Ashraf shared a secret discovery with us, one we were asked not to divulge for another few months. What I am doing right now is not telling you the secret, but that there is a secret that will be announced in the near future. Even though we were told the secret! Isn't that exciting, being in-the-know?

He also told us something that wasn't a secret but did make us feel we were as honored in his country as President Bill Clinton. Ashraf was the guide that took him to the Pharaoh's sarcophagi in the Great Pyramid when he visited here and that he helped him climb into it and lay down just as we had. WOW!

Yet the splendor of our day was only just beginning. The bus waiting at the hotel door with our dutifully accompanying armed guard, took us to the Sondos Papyrus Shop. We were given a very brief show-

Sweet Winds of Egypt

and-tell on the making of the papyrus paper that is produced and sold in their shop. Yet after writing down what notes I could, thinking I might try those instructions using the strange reeds I find growing along my Gasconade River, I wasn't quite satisfied. It wasn't until after I returned to Missouri that I learned from the internet that Papyrus was from its beginning use (sometime in 4000 BC) referred to as the lifeblood for Egypt. This versatile plant was not only used for paper but in the manufacture of ropes, baskets and boats. But the paper revolutionized the way people kept valuable information. It was durable and light weight, and it was being exported from Egypt to the known world of that time.

    We watched the green skin of a pre-cut stalk being removed, the inner pith taken out and cut into long strips. The strips were rolled and pounded and soaked in water. We were shown some that had been soaked for six days and were now a cream color. Leaving them in the water longer would have given them a darker color. They were laid horizontally into the size of the picture that would later be painted on them to sell. Then another layer of strips were vertically laid over the first ones, and both placed between two layers of cotton cloth to help remove the moisture. They were then put into a press to dry and form a single sheet of papyrus paper.

    Later the Arabs developed a process of pulped paper, putting the exporting of papyrus paper into decline. Soon the old secret process was forgotten. It wasn't until

1969 that an Egyptian scientist named Dr. Hasson Ragab reintroduced the papyrus plant, growing it on his plantation near Cairo. Because the exact methods for making good papyrus paper had been kept so secret, there were no written records as to the manufacturing process. But through his experimentation, papyrus paper is making its way back after a long absence.

Because of its uniqueness and the painter's talented and colorful painting on them, I purchased a number of small, yet rather expensive paintings, one for each grandchild. And of course one for myself. Mine portrays three beautiful young women dressed in vibrant blue Egyptian clothing and today hangs in a prominent spot in my library. The beauty of the Ancients is now a part of my life and plays a meaningful role in who I am.

Cairo Egypt

CHAPTER THIRTEEN

THE POWER OF A MUSEUM

The day has already had a full start. It all began with meeting the honored Ashraf, and was followed by the excitement of the Papyrus Store. Can I possibly hold myself together long enough to contain all that is being offered on this buffet of splendor? Ever so quietly, that inbred stamina gene passed down from my forefathers, and most noticeably my foremothers, began to kick in. "Sure I can!"

Statues of Kings and Queens, Gods and Goddesses small and large, paintings, floor tiles, sarcophagi, golden masks and jewelry, thrones, alabaster chests and vases. And oh, not to forget storage rooms filled with hundreds of mummies. All in all there are some 180,000 different artifacts located in this magnificent edifice, The Cairo Museum, built between 1897 and 1902.

Upon entering this open and sky lighted two-story Museum we were able to view one of the earliest created artifacts, a two sided palette called the Narmer Palette, depicting the ruler of the time before the Dynasties were recorded. King Narmer had united Upper and Lower Egypt. That unification was celebrated as a great feat and was shown by the carvings on the pallet with Narmer on one side wearing the white crown of Upper Egypt (resembling a bowling pin) and on the other side, the same King wearing the red crown of Lower Egypt (resembling a chair). And here in front of us was this carved black stone, cut during the first recorded period of Egyptian history around 3000 BC. Blows your mind away, huh? Well it surely did mine!

    It was amazing how Ehab, our registered and quite educated antiquities guide, was able to keep us all herded together as he explained and elaborated on only a couple of hundred of the thousands of artifacts we would see this day. The lower floors were relegated to the treasures from the Old and Middle Kingdoms (approximately 3000 BC to 1,700 BC). The upper floor held the astoundingly fabulous treasures from the New Kingdom, mostly garnered from the unspoiled tomb of King Tut Ankh Amum.

    Somewhere in all of this extensive History lesson I hit on a King that his nation actually chose to despise, calling him after his death a "heretic" for his chosen belief of one God. Somehow it struck a chord within me as I too chose to believe in one God.

    Amenhotep IV, or King Akhenaten, (1353-1335 BC) and his beautiful wife, the long-necked Nefertiti, overwhelmed Egyptian society for about twenty years with their so-called 'religion of Aten". Akhenaten of the elongated face and scull, almond shaped eyes, fleshy lips with hollow cheeks and a prominent chin, left distinctive statues and an altar depicting and characterizing the rich movements of the time in scenes that individualized him and the members of his royal family with their elongated sculls, wide hips and pronounced bellies.

Akhenaten declared that the sun disk "Aten" was the only God and condemned the worship of other deities, removing their names from monuments, abolishing the old priesthoods, closing temples and confiscating their property.

Despite the power of a pharaoh, the politics and power of a wide established priesthood regained their hold on the next ruler in the Pharaoh linage, King Tut, the boy King. And with the discovery in 1922 by Howard Carter of the unbroken-sealed tomb of this boy King, which was located in the Valley of the Kings near the city of Luxor, formerly Thebes, all 500 miles south of Cairo, the treasures found here filled almost the entire second floor of this Museum.

The golden masks, the elaborate gold and jeweled sarcophagus, the ornate jewelry, and the opulent furniture; all these were here on view for me and my new family to explore and enjoy at our own leisure for a period of about two hours. I went back to the stella that was thought to mention the Hebrew people that had once resided here. Interesting.... I viewed again the ageless face of Queen Nefertiti whose name means "Beautiful is coming". Later I purchased a small magnet of her to remind me of her slim beauty each time I open my refrigerator door planning to stuff my fat belly.

It was very hot and stuffy in the museum. While I waited for the time when we would soon gather together at the bus, I found a small bench near the mummy room and leaned back against the cool wall for a fifteen minute power nap. My body and especially my mind can take only so much. This afternoon I had become "overwhelmed" by it all. And yet, everything was just as it should be. I was surrounded by a sweet joy of living.

We had already packed our suitcases this morning storing them under the bus in anticipation of our 6:15 p.m. air flight from Cairo to Luxor. We were allowed to store some of our purchased items at the hotel where we would later spend our last night before our departure from Egypt. This way we would not have to tote them with us during the rest of our journey.

At the hotel we had an hour or so to rest. As today was sweet Jim's birthday, Ruth had purchased a lovely cake for him, decorated with fresh fruit, and topped with a few candles to be lit and blown out with a customary wish. Our laughter filled the lobby as we came to the end of an overflowing day of happiness.

By this time the learning key had been turned off and a passive pleasure in enjoying our newly found comradeship had taken over. Even the hour long flight seemed a breeze; from the quick security line admittance to the already picked up, checked in and stowed baggage.

Sweet Winds of Egypt

On our arrival we were taken to the grandiose Hotel Compound of Sofitel-Karnak where we were royally treated during our stay in the city of Luxor.

Ah, Egypt, now my home away from home, how sweet you are. It was on this day that I decided to put these combined stories into a book form and entitle them, "SWEET WINDS OF EGYPT". Quite fitting, don't you think?

Luxor, Egypt

CHAPTER FOURTEEN

LIFE, NEW ON THE EAST BANK, OLD ON THE WEST BANK

Our breakfast on the open air veranda was extravagant and exciting. A perfect place for romance. What if I were to dream that a discreet love affair could begin, but only in my old, silly mind of course, between this beautiful, young, married with two sons, Egyptian guide and me? He would blow me kisses from his breakfast table. And I would mouth back across the room "I love you". What sweet fun! Never in all my eighty years would I have ever dreamed of being here, much less enjoying fanciful thoughts like this. But it would put a bit of spice in my History Lesson!

Seven is commonly considered a lucky number. It is a dividing number, as in seven days of the week. And today I found it, noting that this is our seventh day in Egypt, to be a busy number. There were seven distinct items on our itinerary that we would view on our "thither-and-yon" travels of the day. We began our New kingdom (1550-1070 BC) experiences here on the west bank, deemed as one of the most famous archeological sites in the world. For they represent the Old Egyptian views of the hereafter and how they buried their dead.

Sweet Winds of Egypt

We were transferred from the Hotel compound by a smaller bus this time as we would be visiting sites where toilets are available (for the usual one-pound coin tip, of course). Ruth arranges to use the big buses that have facilities when we are longer trips.

We were driven first to Deir El Medina, or the workman's village, uncovered only in the past century. There were a few tombs that we were able to visit that held the colorful paintings that are most often pictured in books about Egypt. These tombs were built for the artisans who made the elaborate tombs in the Valley of the Kings and Queens. They were far from being as ornate as the tombs of Pharaohs and Kings, yet they designed their own tombs to display their great talent. This village was the home for these fortunate artists and their families. At the Saqqara compound we saw scenes depicting the daily life during the Old Kingdom. Today we saw paintings of the daily life of the New Kingdom (about 1,000 years later). The path we walked on that overlooked the foundations of the village was strewn with rubble that had been removed from their houses. The important pieces of the discoveries of pottery and household needs had already been removed to be displayed in museums all over the world. But on this path I quietly garnered small pottery shards, tossed away rubble, but still precious to me for my personal pleasure.

Our second stop would deliver us to the Ramesseum. Before we could enter the compound Ehab purchased the needed tickets for admittance. For travelers to visit all the tombs, temples, pyramids and mastabas, it could become quite costly. The charges are usually 30 LE, or approximately $5. And we visited quite a number of them. For some reason this one is rarely visited yet it was a favorite of many of Ruth's groups. The fallen statue of Ramses II had inspired a poem written by Percy Shelly. Pat, our in-group art critic and one who knew her stuff, had obtained a copy of his poem. While on the bus she read it to us. Somehow it strummed another cord in my desert music score, loudly underlining the fact that this Ramses II had once been alive. He was a real person. The inscription on his statue read "I am Ozymandias", (Greek for King of Kings). Actually it's believed he was the pharaoh during the time of Moses and the Exodus. Wow!

And here I was, viewing this statue, lying broken at the entrance to the splendid hypostyle hall and its astrological ceilings. On this day the snapping of hundreds of pictures of numerous Mortuary Temples began. At the end of the trip we shared our digital pictures and between us all, we had some really great shots.

Close to the noon hour we came to our third stop and one of the sweetest for me. We were treated to a fantastic, home cooked family style meal in the long center room of an Egyptian village family. Before I came on this trip I chose to sew up 25 small drawstring bags and place four different American coins in each. They were to be given to the Egyptian children of my choosing. I had already shared about ten of the bags with various children along the way. But today I gave away the remainder to a grandmother letting her distribute them to her numerous grandchildren. I opened one bag to show her what was in them and used a daughter who spoke English to translate for me.

She, and her daughters and daughter-in-laws who live in apartments that are added on to the top of the parents homes, prepared the scrumptious meal. It began with a green lentil soup, and then followed with servings of a baked potato-tomato casserole, big bowls of rice, a tomato-lentil dish, baked chicken and sun bread. Scattered up and down the table were small dishes of assorted dipping sauces. I ate far too much!

Afterwards we had hot tea in their very small courtyard, sitting on hand made couches and benches. The tea was served in small cups with dishes of dried peppermint and raw sugar to compliment the tea. (They grow and process their own sugar cane.) I was again able to visit with the grandmother and had my picture taken with her. I was touched by her profound exchange of love at my gifts for her babies. She cupped her hands around my face and kissed my two cheeks. We were able to exchange how old we were. She was fifty. I told her I was eighty. She was amazed and a bit skeptical but what we both realized was this: being fifty or eighty means nothing. We women maintain our womanhood in ways that have nothing to do with age or nationality. Motherhood in womanhood is all the same.

Near the old capital of Thebes, Egypt

Jeanette Pickering

Resting at the base of the Bent Pyramid

Saqqara Complex with view of the Step Pyramid

Shopping in a Cairo Perfumery

Sweet Winds of Egypt

Meditation between the Sphinx's Paws   Outside the Ramesseum Complex

Young Girls outside the Great Pyramid

Group Picture in front of the Great Pyramid

Jeanette Pickering

Jeanette inside Dier El Medina temple

Women on the steps of Queen Hatshepsut's Temple

Temple of Ramesses II at Abu Simble above High Aswan Dam

Sweet Winds of Egypt

Inside the Philae Temple on Agilaka Island

Shopping at an Egyptian Food Stall in Cairo

Jeanette with a Sweet Egyptian Grandmother

CHAPTER FIFTEEN

A QUEEN WHO WOULD BE KING

Four more steps were needed to complete our seven for this seventh day. And half the day had already been climbed. Ruth had provided us with a hang-around-the-neck pocket in which I carried my pad and pen. I scribbled down notes as if I were going to be tested. Some I knew I would never use, yet this trip was becoming one big beautiful History class and I loved it.

During the afternoon we visited one of the earliest New Kingdom Temples. The purpose of these edifices was to hold the mummified bodies of the Pharaohs and their Queens and to honor their special Gods. And of course to pick up a little recognition for themselves on the way. Of all the temples built by the ancient Egyptians, Queen Hatshepsut's is called "the most splendid of all" by her fellow ancients. This Deir El Bahari edifice has been an inspiration to many founders of modern architecture. It contains three levels with the picturesque columns on the second level being dedicated to her chosen Goddess, Hathor. After climbing the long ramps built in the center of the many steps going up to the newly renovated third level, the view east to the "black land", now green with living growth, presented a breath taking scene. I tried to imagine myself as this powerful queen, gazing out over the small world she then controlled. I doubt that she could have been any happier, with her extreme wealth and power, than I am now. I too am wealthy with the knowledge and world experiences that I have had. I am contentedly grounded in my thoughts of who I am.

Going back down the ramp I was chatting away with my handsome, tattooed friend, Alex, the one we had such fun with in Alexandria where the other girls and I requested, to no avail, to check out his fantastic body art. Near the bottom I tripped. He caught me before I fell.

A small thing, yet in a split second the notes I had written earlier this morning flashed back to my mind. One of the hieroglyphs Ruth had pointed out to us showed a vase holding a heart and a necklace flying up. Its meaning was "when the heart goes wide". My heart had gone wide for this young gentleman who had prevented who knows what kind of a fall I may have taken. What a delightful application to a history lesson.

At a side area roped off and guarded by an armed and uniformed young man, Ehab was able to get us beyond the barriers by sharing a small token of appreciation...their way of doing business. We gathered around one of the ornately inscribed columns and sat on its foundation base while Ehab gave us the reasons for some of the obvious defacements to the carvings of Queen Hatshepsut. It was not only here in her temple we saw them but in other places where her likeness had been desecrated. Many times this was done on command of the ruler that followed out of hateful spite.

Before we left this extraordinary Woman King's Temple, someone suggested a group photo of all the women of our group standing with our arms crossed with the right one over the left just as Queen Hatshepsut would have stood before her people. During our exaggerated posing for the picture a group of Japanese tourists stood behind our men photographers waiting to go up the steps. Well, why not invite those women into our group photo and make this an international woman thing? And so we did. What a jovial bunch we presented. Actually we were just a bunch of giggling girls showing off.

On our way back to the hotel we briefly stopped at the "Colossi of Memnon". There wasn't much there except two large statues of Amenhotep III that still stand even though their temple was destroyed long ago. The Greeks believed they were the statues of Memnon, who was the son of their god, Eros.

We also made a brief stop, our sixth of the day, at an Alabaster Shop where upon entering we were treated to a song-and-shout routine of sorts, introducing us to how the alabaster stone is carved to create the beautiful vases, jugs and statues displayed in their large show room. With my friend Terry's birthday coming up in a few days, I chose to get her something she would like. Since I had only recently celebrated my birthday, we agreed to get matching jars which would hold a tea candle and give them to one another. Fantastic! Now we each think of the other whenever we use them.

Tonight we were to be treated to a trip to the down town Luxor Bazaar area for a shopping spree. So it was back to the hotel for a bit of rest and then get spiffed up for a night on the town.

Deir El Bahari

CHAPTER SIXTEEN

A NIGHT LIFE WITH BARGAINS

Our seventh and final stop on our seventh day in Egypt was the most fun of all. SHOPPING! As I had missed the Cairo shopping trip, choosing to go to Alexandria instead, this Luxor Bazaar trip filled the bill. The day had already been filled with seeing sights but tonight we went hunting for special sights. We were hunting for bargains.

I had showered and put on my loose purple dress for the evening. I wanted to be comfortable as I "negotiated". This would be my best opportunity to pick up gifts for my family for Christmas.

The shops reminded one of a big outdoor sidewalk sale. Tall tables and small tables, covered with scarves, galabeyas, clothing, boxes of whole spices, shelves of ground spices and every conceivable souvenir item you could imagine. But it was the salesmen that you couldn't avoid, each tugging on your arm to come see what he had to sell. Most spoke a smattering of English. The young ones worked so hard trying to charm us with their prowess in using English words.

Sometimes we stayed together as a group. Sometimes we ventured alone into a shop to see what they had inside. I was never afraid and I'm not sure why. The vendors were pests in hawking their wares but never did I have a feeling of unease. I sensed they made sure we were safe—we were their bread and butter.

I shopped for scarves. I've never seen so many beautiful shoulders and head coverings in my life. The designs and colors were astounding. And so inexpensive I was almost ashamed to bargain. But bargaining was a way of shopping here and it became a joyful, playful way of getting, or not getting, the item you wanted.

Ruth taught us how to bargain. She was an expert. Always sweet but firm, even walking away with them following her, haggling a bit more but finally accepting her fair terms. On one occasion when she was with me, she teased the young salesman when I had bought a number of items from his shop, telling him he should give me a gift for my having chosen his shop. And he did. He gave me one of their small coins, one with a hole in the middle. Because their nice one-pound coins, made with a gold colored metal in the center and silver on the rim edge, were worth only twenty cents, I would have guessed this one to be a fraction of a penny. But it was a gift. And it pleased me.

I had to be careful not to buy too many items, inexpensive and beautiful as they were, for I would have to carry them with me for the next seven days. And I had already purchased a small silk rug and some alabaster pieces that were beginning to fill up my suitcase.

Ehab provided the patient father influence, watching over us from the side lines as he sat at an outside

Shisha Bar with his back to the wall, smiling with an amused look as we showed him our purchases. Now and then he would take a puff from his water pipe that smelled so good with aroma of the apple flavored tobacco, shaking his head at our silliness.

I had left a small family shop after purchasing a small souvenir statue and had walked a ways down the street to join some of our group when a young boy, the son of the shop owner came running after me and urging me to come back to the shop. In his broken English he kept saying, "Come. Money. Come." Thinking I must not have paid the right amount, I went back with him to settle it.

His father, who I deemed to be a devout Muslim man because of the dark shadowed bruise on his forehead made by his numerous bowings to the ground to Allah, explained to me that when I paid for my purchase with American dollars, four bills had fallen from my coin purse; a twenty and three ones. He was giving them back to me. Unbelievable!

Of all the things that have happened to me on this trip this one made the biggest impact toward my relationship to these people, this expression of true honesty. It touched my soul. I shared part of it with him. He could have kept it all. But he didn't.

When I put this experience of honesty into the perspective that I now have of what's happening in this man's country today, I can feel and understand their struggle as if I were a part of it. Yes, there are some

Sweet Winds of Egypt

difficult Egyptians, like the man who was just forced out as the leader of Egypt. But there are so many beautiful Godly ones too. They are the ones I support and pray for at this time.

Luxor Egypt

CHAPTER SEVENTEEN

AN UNFULFILLED PILGRAMAGE

Most of the world's major religions will have a focal point or a destination of pilgrimage. It could be a city or a common gathering place where they long to go to at least once in their lifetime. Mecca. Jerusalem. Notre Dame or the Lourdes in France. The Vatican in Rome. For the ancient Egyptians it was Abydos.

Abydos is a town located about a third of the way down the river valley between Luxor and Cairo. Down meaning north. But when history speaks of Abydos it refers to the Temples that are located on the western side in the sands that border the town. Today our excursion would take us there.

Because the past seven days have been long and strenuous, my body is beginning to feel the weariness and stress of the push required. My mind is also feeling the effects of the overload of so much information being given to us by our well educated Ehab. His degree in Egyptology and his experiences in using that degree have made him one of the best guides in Egypt. I just wish I could be a more absorbing student.

On our drive north to reach Abydos we passed through the small city of Nag Hammadi where the famous scroll writings were found in 1945. They were ancient codices dating from 390 AD and contained the gospels of Thomas, Mary and others. I was fifteen at the time they were discovered and remembered the stir it caused, especially in the fundamentalist church which I belonged to at that time. As we drove through the town I thought "This is that place! A piece of history in my own time happened here." Yet what was found reached back so many years it is still difficult for me to fathom.

After hearing Ehab speak of Abydos, as an ancient pilgrimage destination, I came expecting something special to happen to me, but having no clue as to what it would be. Even as I toured the now uncovered, renovated facilities, I picked up shards from the broken pottery pieces scattered outside as pathway gravel and pebbles from the worn rock flooring between the magnificent relief carved columns of this legendary and mysterious Temple built by Seti I in the late 14th century B.C. In their adherences to the worship of the God Osiris, those Egyptians of that time believed that the entrance to the underworld was between the hills of the desert west of the city, thus they built their Temple there.

The Temple of Ramesses II was filled with colorful wall reliefs. It was in a narrow hallway within this temple that the "list of kings" was found. Everyone except me in our group, snapped pictures of this historical reference information wall. I had left my camera on the bus, now parked too far for me to walk back to get it. But once the tour is over we have agreed to share our photos with each other. So I'm covered.

In our brochure this place was listed as "unforgettable" yet I did forget so many things, and later in the trip had to ask Ehab to explain again. I was confused about the temple named OSIREION. Which one was it?" He said it was the one separate and a small distance away from his father's. We had to walk the distance through rough hot desert sand piles, built from fill taken from excavations. This temple was on a lower ground level and when we reached it, we were disappointed to not be able to go inside. Brackish and thick ground water had seeped in from somewhere; I couldn't understand this. In such a dry and arid place where did the water come from? "I'll have to ask Ehab later".

"And what of their calendar of the three seasons of four months of thirty days? (3 x 4 = 12 x 30 = 360 days, not 365). Where are the other five days?"

"Well, they added them in somewhere as five days of religious holidays plus an extra every four years."

Ah Ha! Even the ancients celebrated a leap year!

We returned to the bus where the driver had the air conditioning running so that we were able to eat our boxed lunches in relative comfort. A bit of respite before the trip back and another excursion in Luxor. Some of the others had purchased their lunches ready packed but many of us brought baggies with rolls, cheeses and meats and some fruit from the breakfast buffet.

Sweet Winds of Egypt

I rested as I ate my lunch and mused over my earlier expectation. Had I anticipated a spiritual revelation? Was I expecting an encounter of validation of my belief in the one God? If so, I didn't get it. What I had already received between the paws of the Sphinx would have to suffice for now. I am ready to move on.

Abydos, Egypt

CHAPTER EIGHTEEN

BOOMERANG

The ancient city of Luxor today combines both the past and the present. The present has created accommodations for visitors from all over the world. Crowds of them. Yet the main attraction for those tourist visitors are the pieces of the past, cleared from their timeless sifting of desert sand and restored as faithfully as they can be within limits, to their original grandeur.

Luxor is blessed with so many edifices of antiquity that it is hard to choose from them just which ones would fit into our schedule. But our observant and wisely aware director, sweet Ruth, in her collusion with the ever patient Ehab, have chosen the correct ones for our group. After our hot and dusty morning and afternoon at the Temple of Abydos, the Luxor Temple was a fitting stop to round out our day. For it is in the late afternoon when the sun begins its tilt to the western bank that the lighting on this magnificent secluded compound is at its finest.

Walled off from the main highway that runs along the Nile River to its west, it rests between it and a quieter city street that is pushed up against its eastern boundary. However it still catches the echoes of the city sounds. Because it is so accessible to the tourists, crowds of groups from all over the world had come this evening to

Sweet Winds of Egypt

partake of whatever was offered. Up to now we have been spoiled by having to share our space with only a moderate amount of people. Now they seemed to be everywhere and for Ehab to keep us in check he often called out in his sonorous voice, "Boomerang" which was a name given to our group by the five members who have returned each year to be together.

    This ancient encampment of antiquity was built as a suitable setting for the rituals observed during their Festival of Apet, sometimes listed as Opet, to reconcile the ruler with the divine office. Sound familiar? We do that even today in many of our major religions. But in their time it became the backbone to the Pharaohs' government. Rituals like this are still prevalent today in some of the mideast countries.

    At the time of the sunset, many of the group who had better quality cameras chose to utilize the special lighting effects that bounce off the columns and statues. About four of us wandered to the western side of the enclosure and bribed a guard to be allowed to climb some steps that put us on the ground level with the main highway and the view of the Nile flowing beside it. It gave me a feeling for the enormous amount of labor it has taken to clear out and haul off all the sand and debris from around each structure or statue in this compound. The level of this ancient city is much lower than the level of the city of today. Some of the pictures that are sold in the specialty shops are paintings by the artist David Roberts, done in the year

1838. They show the sand reaching almost to the shoulders of the tallest statues at that time. Placed beside the pictures taken today, they are clearly graphic in their depiction of the work that has been done.

Also excavated along the Nile is an avenue, a canal of sorts, which had at one time held thousands of small sphinx statues. The avenue had connected this temple to the one in Karnak, a city north of Luxor. Today the city-fathers of both towns have seen fit to purchase property along this area and have begun a large renovation project to the point of disrupting normal patterns of business and traffic of this modern day city. But the locals work around the hazards with no problems. They are very aware that excavating these antiquities uncovers their heritage as a value that benefits their livelihood today. Nearly nine percent of Egypt's families are supported by the tourist industry. We who "come to see" are blessed by both those who labor today and those who also labored in the past.

Luxor, Egypt

CHAPTER NINETEEN

BALLOON RIDE ON A MORNING WIND

My night's rest was a short one. This morning I would be awakened the earliest of all my Egypt days; at three fifteen a.m. For at four o'clock we had to be at the small boat docked alongside the street fronting our hotel. We were to break our nights fast with hot tea and cellophane-wrapped sweet breads as we crossed the Nile to the West Bank where our Hot Air Balloon transportation awaited.

Nearly all of our group, plus our faithful Ehab, opted to see the Nile Valley around Luxor from a different perspective. It was still dark as with flashlights we crossed the cool desert sand to where a number of balloons lay flat, waiting to be filled with heated air to lift us, snuggled in the heavy woven baskets, high into the eastern blowing winds. The air had freshness, dry and clear, quite unlike the freshness of the musk of my Ozark forest floor.

We had hoped to be able to look down on the famed Valley of the Kings and the Queens Temple we had visited only a few days before. But they were located in the sands to the west and we were heading east.

The talented Captain of our air boat lifted and lowered his craft with deliberate ease with the squeeze of two levers attached to two tanks of gas that shot bursts of fire to heat the air in the balloon, or pull a rope which activated an opening at the top of the balloon.

We had wanted to ride in the one that sported the spiral rainbow colors, but were given a green and yellow combination. However the one we had wanted would be the one we took pictures of as we sailed the silent, washed blue sky. Our after comment was, "How ironic is that!"

As we slowly sailed over the Nile itself we could look down into its depths to see formations that were only discernable from where we were. I spotted underwater cliffs of white limestone that dropped down into pockets of deep dark green, allowing me to visually measure the depths of this majestic river. Tiny fishing boats dotted its banks where locals harvested their daily food. There were the sail-trimmed Falukas skimming smartly up and down the clear, Sudan mountain-fed liquid thoroughfare.

The reality is you can view only so much of the scenery with your feet firmly planted on the soil. The awesome part is that when you are floating off the ground things are so much more astounding from a birds-eye view.

The housing in the city was mostly apartment complexes with numerous TV satellite dishes perched on the roofs. No cable TV here. I had to wonder, with all the financial aid that we share with this country, how were they still not able to upgrade their communication structure to provide cable service to these people?

Up at the height where we silently cruised along, the city sounds were completely muffled. Yet when the

Sweet Winds of Egypt

Captain lowered the balloon as we crossed over the homes of the farmers at the outskirts of the city we were able to see directly down at their rooftops and into the yards of individual families, hearing the distance-softened bark of a pet dog or the bawl of a penned camel. Just awakened children waved at us and bicycle riders and the old men herding a few goats would ignore us as we passed over them. I imagined they would view us as a nuisance in their busy morning business. As we reached the flat farmland that signals the upcoming desert rock formations and the sand beyond, the Captain began his plans for decent. This air sail was not one in which you could foretell the drop destination with much accuracy. All along we had been guided by the whim of Egypt's winds so by using a radio form of communication he was able to guide the busses holding young men who would, once we hit the ground, stabilize and deflate the balloon. We watched as they man-handled the tough cocoon, pulling, wrapping and tucking it into a big bag. From our basket, now resting in an obviously angry farmer's plowed field we were advised by the captain "Not to worry. He will be compensated."

  A surprise party dance was convened on the spot. And as the young men chose women from our group to dance with them to their singing of Egyptian songs, accompanied by a couple of bongo-type drums, we weren't at all surprised at their first choice: Karen, one of the most beautiful women I've ever met, who is sweet Jim's wife. Now can you guess who was chosen last?

Jeanette Pickering

Undaunted by the young men's obvious lack of recognition of a real old-fashioned jitterbugger, I manipulated the cloddy and chopped cane straw to be twirled by an older, uninterested and low on the list of exciting Egyptian dancers available.

I giggled at the whole unbelieveability of it all. Jeanette Pickering, coming from the Ozark Hills only a week ago and now dancing in a plowed cane field with an unwilling Egyptian man in the Nile Valley of Egypt. What a world!

Luxor Egypt

CHAPTER TWENTY

UNHEARD WORDS FROM SEKHMET

In the darkened dimness, her whiskered mouth silently moved. The long hairs growing beside it were invisible. From the tiny ceiling opening, the entering faint light created an aura of power around her stone cold eyes. And in the silence, Sekhmet spoke unheard words. But only to me. The group of seven of my now bonded friends never heard her silent voice. Yet some how she sent messages to each of us. For one full moment we silently looked into her eyes and received what she had to give. Her message of admonition to me was "Get it done". And I knew then what it was I had to do.

The splendors of Karnak filled our afternoon. Karnak is from the Arabic name meaning "fortified place." In Ancient Egyptian it was "Ipet Isut" meaning "The Most Selected of places" or "Most perfect of places", making this area the center of government during the New Kingdom. Each Pharaoh who took his turn in line tussled to leave a show of impressiveness at Karnak. At its zenith, twelve thousand people lived in this city but no one lived in its temple area. Today it claims the title of holding the largest ancient complex in Egypt.

The Temple of Karnak opens up with a magnificent obelisk, great gates and an unequaled hypostyle hall with multiple temples wandering off from the main passage which runs from west to east. Each temple contained its Pharaoh's appeasement to his personal God. The tiny temple dedicated to Sekhmet was in the northeastern section and had been closed for renovation by the French people who had come to assist the Department of Antiquities in cleaning it. Some in our group wanted to view her temple nook from a pre-chosen desire. Mine came from the simple curiosity I carried with me from the beginning of this trip.

    The area had been roped off, with the last of the afternoon workers leaving the site with the instructions that we were NOT allowed to enter this part of the compound. After their departure, our silver fox approached the guards with a gift, (it's a way of life here) and we were allowed to secretly enter. Quietly, one at a time, we followed him to the darkened chamber where her lioness-likeness stood; alert, open eyed and totally silent.

    My first look into the dim cavern was unimpressive, yet I was by this time in my Egypt experience, able to close off the world surrounding me and open up the shutters of my soul. And that was when she spoke to me, leaving the rest of this day's tour warmed by her light mantle of slow healing as it lay around my shoulders.

    The Botanical Garden, a sacred lake, and a rest stop for a refreshing drink all provided a bandage to cover the Sekhmet salve I had been medicated with. It was at the statue of the Scarab Beatle that I circled its periphery in a clockwise rotation, according to local superstition; three times for a dissolvement of a difficult relationship and then one time around counter clockwise for good luck. Or was the clocking the other way around...I have simply forgotten. I only know that it was with a lighter step that I joined our group to eat at the Karnak Restaurant for yet again another Egyptian feast.

On the bus ride back to the Hotel I was able to review some of the other things I had seen: the fascinating Open Air Museum where the Red Chapel of Queen Hatshepsut and Tutmosis III were reconstructed, and the White Chapel of Senwosret, displayed in raised reliefs and finely carved Middle Kingdom hieroglyphs.

My body seemed to be carrying weariness from all the physical exertion of the day and the spaces in my mind were in overload so all I wanted to do this evening was rest. I opted not to take advantage of the visit to the modern Luxor Museum. As I rested in my room, a poem began forming in my mind. I picked up my always close at hand pad and pen and as the first few words were written, it all began to flow as easy and as peaceful as the silent Nile as it traverses this beloved land. The poem was to be a personal gift to the two beautiful friends who have guided me on this trip.

Yet on reading it at its completion, I knew that anyone who has ever traveled with them could also have these same feelings. And so a few days later I shared it with the group.

Jeanette Pickering

TWO LOVES I LEFT IN EGYPT

When comes the end of a beautiful day,
When my body feels weary and worn,
The song of my soul is sweet and whole,
With a joy of remembrances born.

On wings of pure memories of Egypt fair
And so honest and true to her times
Of ancient and golden wings of warm air
Spun from her rhythmic rhymes,

Spoken from lips of a maiden so fair
With long, shimmering tresses of gold,
And her consort in crime with his silver hair
In their kindness my heart they stole.

And so with the peace that passes all understanding, I closed my eyes and slept soundly for the first time since my arrival in this timeless land.

Luxor Egypt

CHAPTER TWENTY ONE

HOLDING MY HAND

The sun had risen as high as the top of the waving palm fronds that lined the east bank of the Ancient Nile River. Its golden color radiated as a halo as it heralded a lovely, cool Egypt morning. This day would present to me the sights and experiences I have waited for since I was a child, reading about this country from my third grade Geography book. A boat ride down the Nile River.

Because there was no rush on time this morning we could sleep a bit later or spend a few more minutes at the cloth-covered breakfast tables outside on the veranda overlooking the Nile. It was during these personal moments of comradeship that we shared the stories of our back home lives, allowing us to know each other more fully.

I carried a satchel containing my notebook and pen, a hat and scarf and my shoulder bag. We were bused to the large excursion boat "La Lotus" and began a leisurely glide down the timeless Nile, north to the lower country where we had begun our trip ten days ago. The water was dark olive-green in color. Looking across to the banks of this river, the easiness in the pace of Egyptian life resembled our slow plying of the water. We watched the scenes of local lives scroll out. Views of today's farm life, having barely changed through the centuries, gave us individual experiences to take in and absorb as memories. Each would filter our own discovered things with our own particular sieve and later would share the resulting treasures with the one another.

I had chosen a vacant seat on the eastern side of the deck, next to a Belgian family which included Lanny, a sweet young boy of five and his sister, Sasha who was eight. They knew a smattering of English and we visited about their coloring books and my writing pad that kept us occupied to break the monotony of farm after farm. Many of our group sat in clusters, chatting and laughing, swapping jokes and stories.

We were served lunch in a large downstairs dining room, also on cloth-covered dining tables. Back in the U.S., I denote eating at a table covered with cloth as a bit of elegant dining. And on this trip I attest to have eaten quite elegantly.

Having spent the past ten years of my life sailing on a small vessel, I was able to detect with a measure of instinct whether our speed was propelled by a motor or by the flow of the water. Our destination point in miles wasn't far down the river so I judged we were using the current to make our way down to Dendera where we would disembark and be taken by bus to the Temple of Hathor.

In its earliest existence this spot in the desert had supported a place of worship for the goddess Hathor. Her hieroglyph denotes a house or womb with Horus inside and her sacred animal is a cow. Later in the

Ptolemaic era the Greeks built a Temple on the same site to honor her. Its ceilings and walls are full of astrological imagery. Through the ages the structures became covered with dark soot and just recently, renovations have cleaned them up and have restored their breath-taking vibrant colors.

During part of our tour of this place, Ehab led us up to a chapel room on the roof of the temple where a famous circular zodiac had been created on the ceiling. The original ceiling was removed centuries ago. In 1820s it was carried off by the Frenchman Jean-Baptiste Lelorrain to Paris. It was later replaced with one fashioned as identical to the original as it could be. The Egyptian government continues to request its return, as well as asking other countries who have taken away the artifacts they found, to return them too.

I had worn a sleeveless long dress with a scarf for my shoulders and a wide brimmed hat for my head. And when allowed a time of private exploration or rest, I chose rest. A three foot base for an absent statue located in a shady spot provided a sweet respite. This quiet spot gave me a chance to reflect on my travels here. And despite all my efforts to put aside the heart ache I was experiencing over my separation from the Captain, in this moment of solitude it rushed back in as a fresh breeze: that wanting to be back on our small boat sailing the Caribbean again.

The wise Ehab sat on the steps of the Temple doorway, waiting for his scattered flock to return to the shepherd. He sensed my discomfort from a distance, calling to me to see if I needed company. "No, I'm o.k."

The others began their trek back to the distant parking lot. Ehab came over to where I was sitting, took my hand and walked the entire route back holding it tightly but with such gentleness I felt my heart would burst with the concerning love he was sending my way.

I've heard of the Agape love; a special self-giving loyal concern that freely accepts another and seeks his or her good. So many search their whole lives for a taste of this kind of love. Today it came to me from a young Egyptian man, wise beyond his years. What a blessing.

Nile River, Egypt

CHAPTER TWENTY TWO

A GREEN FACIAL

It was still mid-afternoon when we began our return to Luxor, this time motoring back south up the river. On the bus back from the Dendera Temple to our cruise liner "La Lotus", we were joined by Lanny and Sascha with their parents in the two spare seats that were vacant. Our excitement was a bit more subdued but none-the-less jovial. I need a lot of laughing right now.

Back on the ship we were served tea on the upstairs deck. This was a sweet treat, sipping tea and eating cake, sitting in the same place but now on the cool side of the deck. I did some more writing. A young man, who seemed quite pleasant, had set up a couple of tables loaded with scarves, shawls, books, and trinkets of all kinds. He had two seats by his tables so I walked over and sat in one. We visited. He gave me his name but I have forgotten it. He was a family man, with a loving wife (and he really adored her, I could tell) and two small children. He had no customers and I had plenty of free time so we chatted about his life here in Egypt.

Ruth had cautioned us that some of the people we would meet would not be our "friends" as they would try to portray themselves, just to make a sale. So I was reserved in my feelings, yet I listened to him and shared happenings of my life with him. Our conversation, I soon realized, was not to make a sale. He was truly sharing with me the struggle of the ordinary Egyptian man to keep his family together and bread on the table in the economy of Egypt of today.

I returned to my deck seat and mulled over the many items he had on his tables, weighing their price, judging if they would make good gifts or could be used simply for my own pleasure. I made a few notes; then went back, chose some nice scarves, a lovely shawl for myself and had some small cartouches ordered for the grandchildren. I also chose a nice book of history with picture's of Egypt. I explained I did not have enough cash with me but could charge them to my Visa Card.

What wasn't made clear was that he couldn't take my Visa card on the boat. After I made my choices, I then learned I would have to go on shore after we docked, to the ATM Bank Machine and using my card there, get cash for him. When I finally realized what would have to be done, I knew from time constraints that I would not be able to do this. So I would just use what cash I did have to pay for the ordered caroches and forget the rest. Yet by now I wanted the rest. I would just have to figure out a way.

One of my friends offered to loan me what cash he had until we got back to the hotel. I also remembered a hidden bill I always carry in my I.D. pouch. That would be enough. So I paid for my treasures and left a bit flustered and stressed over the whole transaction, yet confident that

I had made wise choices in what I had done. There have been times when in the haste of shopping, I have not.

Our day ended in a bus trip back through the city to our hotel. Waiting at a stop in the flow of the traffic, from my window seat I was able to view into a local barber shop. Our wait lasted long enough for me to watch the scene of a barber putting the finishing touches on a green face mask he had applied to a young suit-dressed gentleman and then lifting up the barber chair, turned him around to look into the faces of the people on a bus, watching him. His look back was incredulous. Astounded and totally surprised to see an old woman smiling and waving to him.

This time the Egyptian impression of the American tourist was not so much of "the Ugly American" but what "a stupid bunch of people" we are. It was a delightfully hilarious ending for my day.

Luxor, Egypt

CHAPTER TWENTY THREE

THE GRAVEYARD OF KINGS

Today would be the last day for all of us being together. Three of our group will leave early tomorrow morning to return to the states. So our plans for this day are to make it as special as we can for all of us.

It began with our usual sharing of a buffet breakfast on the Hotel veranda. I snipped a yellow flower from the bounteous supply growing over the ledge beside our table and tucked it behind my ear. Later I pressed it and brought it home for my scrapbook.

Today our search for adventure is in one of the most famous archeological sights in Egypt: the Valley of the Kings where in 1922 Howard Carter found the sealed tomb of King Tutankhamen. Over sixty-two tombs have by now been located here with more still hidden away from the curious, present-day archaeologists.

In this amazingly small twisting valley, dry as a proverbial bone, not a well of water or any green growth can be found here in this grave yard. Only thirty-two of the sixty-two tombs are for Kings. It is not clear who the rest are for. Possibly VIP's and other special people who were leaders under the Pharaohs in those ancient times.

The joint tomb of Ramesses V and VI has just recently been restored back to its breathtaking beauty using newly pioneered modern techniques. We were given vouchers to enter this tomb and three others of our choosing. The morning heralded another hot day so we chose to spend our time in the cool tombs.

With the hieroglyphs and paintings previously covered with the dust from the valley, now restored to their original vibrant colors, the joy of seeing the brilliant blue cobalt color of the ceiling was astounding, knowing that it had been painted there thousands of years ago. The stories told of the lives of these two Kings simply boggled my mind. Their mummies and traveling treasures were not there, of course, for they had been stolen or carried off goodness knows how many years ago.

It was hard to determine just which tombs to pick out to visit. We had all gone together to view the painting treasures of Tomb #9. We then split into smaller groups depending upon who wanted to go where. I bought a small map which showed the locations and name notations of each tomb. There were crowds of visitors here but with so many different choices to pick from, most everyone could move at their own pace, spending as much time as they wanted in any given tomb.

It was important for Pat, the one member of our group who was Jewish, to choose to concentrate her thoughts in the tomb of the Pharaoh who had been the ruler in the time of the Hebrew exodus from Egypt.

Toni and I paired off and chose #15 where Seti II had once been entombed. We then viewed the tomb of Siptah, #47. I'm not sure how the numbering sequence was established but these two were fairly close together. Inside #47, a young man joined us. He was traveling alone through Egypt and staying at the inexpensive Youth Hostels that are provided by the cities. His name was Casey and he was from South Dakota.

I needed to sit a spell and get a cool drink so while Toni took off on another excursion, Casey and I rested at a centralized open air café where he ate a bite, dutifully counting his expenditures used from a frugal budget. I had some extra fruit bars that I always carry and shared them with him.

Accompanied by Casey, my last tomb invasion was in Tomb #11 where Ramesses III had once been buried. It was a small one located close to the café. It was getting close to our departure time so after about ten minutes, I chose to return to our gathering place and rest and reflect on all I'd seen and experienced.

This Valley was sacred to the Goddess Mereseger who in most of the tombs is depicted in carvings of a woman with a cobra's head. Her name means "She who likes silence" and her spirit had begun to resonate within me as I found the weariness of the passing days settling over me. I craved a moment or two of silence and aloneness with which to break the momentous push to see as much as I can while I am able. I found a bench, leaned back, closed my eyes and for a brief while shut out this noisy world, and easily slipped into Mereseger's silence.

Valley of the Kings, Egypt

CHAPTER TWENTY FOUR

TEMPLES, TACKING SAILS AND TEARS

Temples are different from tombs. And each serves its own special purpose. Tombs are for burials. The Valley of the Kings had provided a perfect place for burial tombs, tucked and hidden back into the sides of a secluded sandy trough. But temples were built as tributes from the ruling King to honor his own particular god or goddess. The last great temple built while Egypt was ruling supreme was the Medinet Habu Temple.

It was a fitting stop for the afternoon. You might call it the big test in our history class. The hall of pillars of this compound contained so many beautifully colored reliefs and paintings that we have learned about. We were asked to identify as many as we could and amazingly, we knew many more that we realized.

By this time our group had become well-bonded friends and today a faint, dim, sorrowful cloud tagged behind us. We knew that tonight three of our family would be leaving to fly back to the states. And all three had played important parts in this Egypt stage play. Alex had become my special dark-haired, tattooed Adonis. Toni was my adventurous wandering partner. And Christine, a healer, had helped provide the guidance and healing that I had needed.

This Habu Temple was built by Ramesses III, whose tomb we visited this morning. It had been built on a site seeded by the Woman King, Hatshepsut. In this temple many of the hieroglyphics were carved deeply into the stone. Ehab was able to place his hand into the one of Ra, the sun god.

It was in this temple that I met two more precious children, also from Belgium. Louis was writing his name with chalk on the dirty stone that formed our walkway. "Is this your name?" I asked. "Yes." "And what is the name of your sister?" "She's not my sister, only family." His English was very clear and understandable.

I turned to her to ask her name. "Clementine." she replied, "but my father's name is Louis too." I told them I had left my car in the USA at a town called St. Louis. Then I told them my name, "Jeanette". Louis smiled and said "It is beautiful!" Oh what a heart throb this young man will be! He already knows how to pluck a woman's heart strings.

There was still an hour or so before sunset and a few of us wanted to board the small felucca boat that takes passengers out onto the river where we would be able to view the close of day. I so long to go back to the sailing I love yet I pretty well know that this part of my life is over. But to have an opportunity like this, to sail on the Nile in a

Sweet Winds of Egypt

boat about the size of ROSA, comes only once in my lifetime.

This felucca was a chunky, old wooden boat with an old patched sail. It was maneuvered by a long handled rudder and a long pole to fend us away from the shallows. The Captain was an older man who sat cross legged on the area from which he steered. His son, who spoke broken English, was his mate. I tried to tell them I once lived on and sailed a small boat in the Caribbean Sea. They understood enough to ask if I would like to take the helm for a bit. "Yes, I would like that."

It was far more clumsy than my sleek little boat ROSA, but it wasn't too difficult to manipulate in such calm, unreefed water. At the moment the sun slid behind the western sand we watched for the green flash. Somehow I didn't expect one. The atmosphere above the desert sand is not the same as over an expansive salty sea where I was blessed to see quite a few.

By this time our Boomerang group had now shared so much of the total Egyptian experience that we were able to weave and tie our silk-thread colors of remembrances into the warp of the red and black sands and soil of this Beloved Egypt. We have been woven into a beautiful carpet, fit for Powerful Kings and Petite Queens to walk on. And on this evening of goodbyes we each shared a small piece of our experiences with the others.

Pat had created hand written awards for each of us, reading them out loud and presenting them to us with such loving expression. I read the poem I had written a few days before. We hugged and cried and followed our departing three out to the waiting bus to take them to the airport. As they pulled out of the driveway, those of us left behind sang the farewell song of the Von Trap singers to send them on their way.

But the evening wasn't over yet. Tired as I was I still had to repack my suitcase before going to bed. Tomorrow we are leaving Luxor to head to Upper Egypt and the Aswan Dam. There is still much more that beckons us to "Come see".

Luxor, Egypt

CHAPTER TWENTY FIVE

AND THE HISTORY LESSONS CONTINUE

Oh, the joy of a glorious Egyptian morning. My already packed bags were set outside the door. The bulging carry-on was toted down to the breakfast area. And another omelet meal was savored. This would be the last time we would eat on this balcony veranda overlooking the Nile.

Our bus ride south took us through the metropolis of Luxor, giving us our last look into the small alleyway passages between the "come buy" shops. Children, dogs and assorted adults were leaving their apartment homes to begin their morning activities.

Today we are traveling to where the Nubian people live. They are not quite Egyptian or African but somewhere in-between and now that the new Aswan Dam has been built, a good deal of their homeland has been covered by water.

The two hour morning ride, always climbing in small increments of altitude, will be taking us farther into the ancient Upper Kingdom. The city of Luxor is also considered to be in Upper Egypt. In fact in ancient times anything south of Cairo was in Upper Egypt. On this road I received my first view of the cemeteries of modern burials. No grass grows in these graveyards. I found them plotted and lined in areas similar to the grave spacing in the States. Simple, thin markers identify the people buried under the mounded piles of sand.

It was 9:30 when we arrived at the Edfu Temple, halfway between Luxor and Aswan. This temple was dedicated to the God Horus and was built in the Greek Ptolemaic Period around 237 BC, after the days of the Pharaohs. It was not really discovered until the later years of the 1800's. Then only after removing the inhabitants that lived over the site, could the excavating of the sand and garbage be done. It was much later that the mystic ancient structures could be cleaned to accommodate the new tourist visitors.

Mud brick walls had been built to surround the compound. We noticed the elongated slots that were cut into the granite front of a temple from which staffs with flags could be hung. At one time a huge, very tall door protected the entrance. It was opened only when religious ceremonies for the people were celebrated. The priests always entered from two side entrances. There were thirty-two columns in the courtyard. Just on the inside wall of the entranceway we found the carving of a King being given the Key of Life. To the right of the entrance was a small room called the Vestry where jars of ointments had been kept. To the left was a small Library where at one time parchments were stored. Hieroglyphic catalogue inscriptions were cut in the wall.

Sweet Winds of Egypt

There were more rooms expanding out from the courtyard. Some were storage rooms. One wore a hieroglyphic sign telling that it was a Perfumery, with recipes for the scented oils carved in the walls. There were other carvings showing the hieroglyphs for numbering.

All of this was built and inscribed during the time when the Greeks ruled Egypt. The theme of the stories in this temple was the seventeen year battle between the god Horus and his adversary, his evil uncle Seth who had killed his father. Seth was depicted as a hippopotamus and many scenes showed him being speared by Horus. In this battle, Horus lost an eye. The thing that I found so interesting about this is that the hieroglyphs marking this lost eye have through time evolved into the symbol denoting the R X on our prescriptions, something I had never noticed before.

Here, as in most of the temples or tombs where the God of Fertility, Min has been depicted, his male organ is always shown in the state of erection. Through the years men have chipped at these raised-relief carvings, converting the chips into dust and ingesting them as a form of Viagra. My comment on this is that I'm not sure men have changed much through the years!

The aura inside this Temple held a strong emotion of evilness. Later, when we had finished our tour through this temple, we discussed what our moods were and how we felt as we walked around inside this enclosure. Many had felt agitated and aggravated. And strangely enough, according to the guides this was a common happening. Ah, the unseen power of ancient Temples.

Before the day had come to an end, our bus stopped once more, to visit the Kom Ombo Temple. It was not in as good a condition as the others. It was called a Double, as it contained two identical sides, all under one roof and dedicated to two different, get-along gods. It was built between the years 198 BC and 200 AD and became the gold trade center in Roman times. The two gods were Sobec, a crocodile, and an aspect of Horus, a hawk. In this temple the carvings tell the story of their calendar, made of three seasons. The flooding of the Nile, the planting season and the harvesting season. Each season contains four months. Each month was made up of three weeks consisting of ten days each.

Because of the date of its construction, the carvings showed both the likenesses of the Roman Emperor "TRAJAN" and of IMHOTEP, the Egyptian god of medicine.

I enjoy seeing and learning about the ancient days of Egypt but I also enjoy the Egypt of the present. When the bus pulled up to a beautiful Hotel build on a hillside in Aswan I found the blessing of another comfortable bed. It was to give me a good nights rest in preparation for tomorrow's long, tiresome ride through the desert.

Aswan, Egypt

CHAPTER TWENTY SIX

THE WOMAN IN THE MIRROR

I was awakened on this brilliant morning by the sound of birds singing from the trees that grew in a semi-circle around the pool below the balcony of the room that Terry and I shared. Dreams and sweet thoughts had accompanied my sleep. In fact, at one point during the night I awoke from a dream that I wanted to remember again and got up to get my pad and pen to write down the special items that had pleased me so much. Actually this whole trip has been a bit of a dream that I don't want to wake up from.

I got up on my second awakening, filled with new strength and with the knowledge that my spirit is now being rejuvenated day by day. The lovely little balcony overlooking the large blue water pool beckoned me to come out and sit a while. So I did.

During the days of rushed moving along I have not allowed myself to backslide into thoughts of the recent past. But upon seeing an early, lone swimmer dive into the pool and begin a beautiful crawl stroke across the clear water, I could see the bronzed, strong arms of my lover moving away from me, then back to me and then again, away. If there was any backsliding, this morning it felt right. And I did go back for a bit, remembering places so opposite from this desert land that I am now traveling through.

It is always sweet to wake up on a birthday morning, no matter who you are or what your age. Today I wanted my roommate, Terry, to have her best one yet. If it had not been for her, I would never have found myself in this fabulous part of the world to celebrate her special day. I appreciate her more that she can know.

Our breakfast room today was inside, filled with people from a half-dozen other countries, all of us chatting up a storm. More cloth-covered tables and buffet food prepared by a different set of cooks. This morning we were allowed time to enjoy our breakfast hour with ease as leaving time would be later than usual.

After breaking our night's fast Terry and I walked up to the roof top to look over the city of Aswan and a bit of Lake Nasser in the distance. Life is so good.

When we left the Hotel we joined in with a convoy of buses traveling across the open desert, stretching out the hours, riding up a long, small, two-lane asphalt highway to our destination, Abu Simbel. We traveled convoy style not because of terrorists but because of bandits who will often appear out of nowhere from the desert, to assault a lone bus.

Ruth came prepared for Terry's birthday with a small chocolate cake decorated with items denoting the past, present and future. It gave the trip a festive party atmosphere. We sang. We chatted, with laughter spilling out all over the place. We shared our personal lives with each other. Ehab had brought his computer which held pictures of his "movie star wife" and his two twin boys. I dug out my small picture album containing my special pictures of my Caribbean sailing.

During the noontime when the sun was at its peak, the shimmering of the desert mirages were strong. In the back drop were humped mounds of dark grey stones that when seen past the mirage, their images became reflected in the mirage itself. If one did not know it, the scene could definitely give the impression of a lake of water in this vast, dry, desert sand.

As the earth whirled, the sun was moved from the east to the west and now began to stream in through the western windows of the bus. My chosen seat was on the east side of the bus which was now in the shadows and not quite so blinding and hot. Our bus was provided with a very small, compact toilet area. As I used the facilities and stood to wash my hands, a strange thing happened to me. I quickly returned to my seat somewhat in a daze of enlightenment. Very strange. I wrote down what had happened as if composing an assignment to be read in class. Which is actually what did later occur. Many of us took turns to come to the front of the bus where there was a microphone. In a public moment of sharing, I read my written introspection.

"On this lovely afternoon, moving caravan fashion through the Upper Desert, I had an opportunity to greet the new Jeanette. In the mirror of the tiny closeted toilet on the bus, I saw her. And I was even startled by her beauty. The soft pale blueness of her eyes, the golden rose of her cheeks, and even the softness of her mouth with its smile-wrinkles took me by surprise. So much so that I had to talk to her.

Was it only a few weeks ago that I spoke to the old Jeanette; she who was still depressed, wallowing in the knowledge of having been used, abused, still clinging to the one who had captivated her by his neediness? When I looked into the mirror back then, I hated who I saw, spitting at her with vicious words, shaming her for her stupidity, her naiveness, and her weakness.

Today, that woman was gone. And the woman who had emerged radiated with joy. I immediately fell in love with her. I want to live with her for the rest of my life. And I told her so!"

The Upper desert of Egypt

CHAPTER TWENTY SEVEN

LIGHTS AND SOUNDS AND PEEPING TOMS!

The long desert road on which we traveled today is the same one that will be shown on our nightly news a month from now. For it wasn't until I had returned back to the states that I was shown how truly dangerous this road could be. The news footage showed another tour bus lying on its side with half of the bus shorn off. Half of its occupants, touring visitors just like us, were dead. However they had been taking the night convoy and had hit a truck parked half on, half off the road. Sometimes these convoys drive in the dark without headlights using the open desert light to see by. Our Ruth chooses not to use the night convoys for her tours.

There is no doubt that many catastrophes have happened on this lonely road and it makes one wonder. So when our trek along this uninhabited, unfoliaged stretch with its washed-out pale blue sky ended, we were relieved to arrive at our Hotel in Abu Simbel.

We are only thirty five kilometers from the Sudan border with the newly formed Lake Nasser beginning to create a new delta area here in Upper Egypt. The building of the old Aswan Dam in the later 1800's was profitable for those times but the new one built in 1960 is seventeen times higher even than the Great Pyramid, flooding parts of the unusable desert to create greater opportunities for the Egypt of today.

One of the drawbacks when building this dam was that the huge river-level Temple built by King Ramesses II for himself and the one for his wife, Queen Nefertari, would be covered by the formed lake. One has to wonder why this King, who lived much farther down on the river, would build such an edifice in this place. Yet the carvings, paintings and hieroglyphics we saw this afternoon gave us a clue. It is now supposed that he wanted to warn the people of Southern Nubia that he was the King here and would tolerate no encroachment onto his land. Long strings of shackled slaves were depicted along with other various warnings.

To see its ancient elegance disappear under the Nile waters could not be allowed to happen so a foundation of interested world wide countries helped UNESCO assist the Egyptians in moving the statues and edifices up to a higher man made cliff-plateau and thus preserve an invaluable piece of history. It was an amazing labor of that Agape love which I had found here earlier in our trip. Love of antiquities. Love of history. Love for the people who would profit in so many ways by the move.

We viewed this relocated historical compound in the late afternoon after the crowds had dispersed. Without having to jostle for a place in line or hurry to accommodate others behind us, we were able to move at our leisure and to absorb the sights.

The room assigned to Terry and me was on a lower level, closer to the lake water, with a motel-like atmosphere. Within its tranquility, the short nap I was able to catch was easy and sweet. By the time the sun had set and the soft warm air of evening had begun to stir, our group gathered to walk down to the ampi-theatre. We were pleasantly surprised to run into Libbie who had left our group yesterday to board a Nile River Cruiser that would travel back down the river where she would join a friend in Cairo for a few more days of Egypt Splendor. She was able to sit with us as we were treated to a review of the history of time so long ago with lights of alternate color illuminating the four colossal statues of Ramesses II fronting the lifted cavern of carvings behind them. Then, with the sonorous voice of an English actor speaking into the earphones that had been provided, we heard the story of both the meaning of the Temples and the immensity of the labor it had taken to move them. As the voice continued its professorial history lesson, the swaying of the light from Ramesses' Temple to Queen Nefertari's Temple, along with the monotony of the sound, activated a desire in me to return to the resting nap I had coaxed myself out of earlier. We were beginning to burn our candle at the opposite end now.

Jeanette Pickering

During our late meal we were able to share tokens of our affection with our birthday girl and then wearily we wandered back to our waiting beds.

We locked the door and pulled the drapes to silence and darken the room. At around midnight, I, sleeping in the bed next to the door, was awakened by a faint scratching sound coming from the door. I was startled but not alarmed. I listened. The sound did not go away. Then through a crack at the drapes I saw a bit of flickering light. So strange... I got up and slowly, softly pulled back the curtain covering the door pane. My Word! We had a peeping Tom!

When I finally opened the door, there was a very startled Tom Ross, kneeling in front of the door with is lighter flickering to find the correct way to insert his card-key, thinking this was his room. We all laughed heartily with the humor of it all. I think Tom was the most startled. And embarrassed. We teased him unmercifully about it later. He had simply gone to the swimming pool during the night and then misplaced his room.

Thinking back to these adventures creates a loving longing for these friends. Will I ever see them again? I truly hope so.

Abu Simbel, Egypt

CHAPTER TWENTY EIGHT

AND SO I SING, "THANK YOU"

A somber mantle of realization hovered over us all this day. To realize the end of our shared association was so near caused a disturbing ache in my soul. I don't relish goodbyes. Yet they are necessary as a part of living, to be able to say a new hello. I know that.

We were again placed into a long caravan of chartered busses to traverse back across this desolate sand, which today seemed even more forlorn. Our bus was asked to caboose this desert train as it was one of the bigger ones and we had less passengers, allowing extra room in case a smaller one would break down.

We were traveling back to Aswan where at seven this evening we would fly back to Cairo and ultimately back to the states. But for one last time we had the opportunity for a small intimate group gathering for spiritual uplifting before dispersing back again into our old lives. The chosen place for our final circling of souls was in the beautiful Philae Temple. It too had been dismantled and moved from its original place to higher ground because of the Dam.

Its various shrines and sanctuaries were now located on Agilika Island, thus we had to be transported there by a small, noisy and black-exhaust motor boat. But the place itself was a quiet, serene oasis surrounded by the water of the Nile which had widened out lake-like between the older Low Dam and the new High Dam as it slapped against the rocky banks.

We first toured the place as a group with a final history lesson from our Ehab and then each could choose to wander at their own pace. I chose to roam alone, wandering through an area of uncleared sandy soil. As I walked I picked a small wildflower and put it behind my ear. I gathered random pebbles, putting them in my pocket for sharing with my friends back home.

I found a special feeling here. Having been led by the goddess Sekhmet to "get it done", to clean out my unhappiness, I was now able to absorb the spirit of the goddess Isis to whom this temple is dedicated. She represents everything beautiful and is the protector of both mothers and their children. In my openness of spirit, I could view her as a prototype of Mary, the mother of Jesus. Just as sweet Mary has reached out to all mothers, Isis too had reached out to me. I kept in mind that the "One God" might be peeved with me for bypassing Him, but I still asked her to protect me as I move on and along this new path for my life. Surely he wouldn't frown on that.

Our meditation time came at the end of our visit here. We were on the steps leading down to the water on the east side of the island. I had already gone down to dip my hands in the water and wash my face. I gathered two beautiful flat rocks from the water and tucked them into my bag. The spiritual moment today consisted of simply sitting on the steps and looking out over the water, then with the joining of hands, we silently thanked each other and bid our goodbyes.

It was at the airport that I realized just how much this trip meant, not only to me but to the others. As Ruth downloaded my pictures and ones the others had taken onto her computer, she and I visited. She showed me a beautiful gold ring that Judy had slipped on her finger only moments before. She had also shared one with Ehab. Judy may have wanted this to be a secret but it was too special for Ruth not to share.

This lovely woman, Judy, who had been almost unapproachable to me in my mind because of her sweet manner of being such a beautiful Lady, had in my view, this time up-Oprahed even Oprah herself in her generosity. The emotional heaviness of her gift, weighed tons. Her generosity inspired and motivated me to evaluate my own generousness and to produce a higher value in my giving.

This entire Egyptian episode has opened in me a new way to look at my world with the result of also opening unused resources of evaluation of my own soul. Thus to whatever god or goddesses that may be out there, who might be listening to me at any given time, I sing out "Thank You!"

Philae Temple

CHAPTER TWENTY NINE

HOMEWARD BOUND

We had arrived back at the Hotel by the airport last night in time to regroup and repack our bags before I dropped into bed fully clothed and ready to catch the shuttle bus at 2:00 a.m. Lisa, Terry and I were the only ones of our group to make this flight out. Lisa, a smart little lady, had very little luggage to bog her down. I had ample but was able to get it checked and cleared without a hassle. With only two hours of sleep I was ill prepared for the chauvinistic hassle that we had to face as they checked Terry's luggage. It really tried all the patience we could muster to deal with the mindset of this Egyptian male superiority.

The first challenge began when Terry placed her suitcase on the roller belt of the X-ray machine. She had purchased a four bottle set of rose oil at the Perfumery. These oils are so very expensive in the U.S. and so economical here in Egypt. They were packed in a beautiful, blue velvet chest, well packed and protected against breakage. For one full hour, four know-it-all gentlemen took their time in determining the contents were what she said they were.

Then came the problem of the qualitative description of what a carry on bag could be and the amount

Sweet Winds of Egypt

of weight it could contain. They tried to charge her VISA card an extra $200. U.S. dollars for a few kilograms over the 12 allowed. She refused to pay it, and requested that they return her checked baggage so she could remove the few kilos that made it over-weight and place them in the checked luggage. She may have let it pass if it hadn't been such an exorbitant amount they were trying to get from her.

Finally the bags were re-checked and we were allowed into the secure area with only a few minutes to spare before getting to the boarding gate for our flight to Amsterdam. This was Egypt at its worst. Security, we realize is necessary and so we put up with the aggravation.

After being seated with our belts fastened for the take off, we had a chance to see that it wasn't the rules that had upset us but the disorganization and unpleasantness we received from the men policing those rules.

Our plane routing home took us through the Netherlands where the young women who checked our carry-on baggage and gave us our required pat-downs, worked with smiles and pleasantness as they completed the same tasks as the Egyptian men had yet with such a different mind-set. Makes you wonder.

The three of us separated in New York. Our goodbye was not tearful—we were all simply too tired to even cry. My hop to Minneapolis and then to St. Louis gave me hours of quiet-mind reflection time. Even on a noisy and crowded airplane. I chose to surround myself with aloneness and was able to look back on this trip as an extraordinary adventure, one of a lifetime. I was able to relive it by writing it down with all the good and the bad, the sadness and the laughter. If there was even a hint of animosity felt among us in these shared days, I couldn't see for all the love that was there.

Now, here I am at the end of this long, stretched out day with the weights of my Grandmother Clock hovering at the bottom link of their chains. With a sweet awareness of mind, there comes creeping in on the periphery, a softened old soul. It was that woman who could condense into a small simple package, all those years she had spent on the Caribbean Sea, living on her beloved boat ROSA with her jumble-wired Captain. That was when I caught my breath and understood.

What I now realize, have accepted and must acknowledge is this: Egypt was fantastic. I would recommend a trip there with Ruth and Ehab to anyone with an adventurous nature. But nothing, not even Egypt, can replace those Caribbean Sea days as the most adventurous segment of my life. I loved the desert, the Ancient. But I miss the Captain and the Sea.

The End

www.ingramcontent.com/pod-product-compliance
Lightning Source LLC
Chambersburg PA
CBHW072011290426
44109CB00018B/2209